I0829574

Supply and Demand

Why Things Cost What They Do

Alfred Greene

Copyright 2024 Alfred Greene. All
Rights reserved. No part of this publication
may be reproduced without the consent of the
author.

"Teach a parrot the terms 'supply and demand' and you've got an economist."

--Thomas Carlyle

Alfred Greene

Table of Contents

Introduction

Have you ever wondered why the price of your favorite coffee suddenly skyrockets, or why that trendy gadget you've been eyeing becomes surprisingly affordable overnight? These everyday mysteries are rooted in the fundamental economic principles of supply and demand. Welcome to "Supply and Demand: Why Things Cost What They Do," your guide to unraveling the hidden forces that shape the prices we encounter in our daily lives.

Imagine you're at a bustling farmer's market on a sunny Saturday morning. As you browse the stalls, you notice that strawberries are unusually cheap this week, while avocados are priced higher than ever. What's going on? The answer lies in the delicate dance between supply and demand, a concept that governs not just fruit prices, but the entire global economy.

In this book, we'll explore how these economic forces work behind the scenes, influencing everything from your morning latte to the cost of your dream home. You'll discover how businesses set prices, why some products become scarce while others flood the market, and how your own choices as a consumer play a crucial role in this intricate economic web.

By the time you finish reading, you'll have a new lens through which to view the world. You'll understand the subtle economic signals that surround us and how they affect our daily decisions. Whether you're a student, a professional, or simply curious about the workings of the marketplace, this book will equip you with valuable insights to navigate our complex economic landscape.

So, are you ready to unlock the secrets of supply and demand? Let's begin our journey into the fascinating world of economics, where every price tag tells a story, and every purchase you make shapes the market in ways you might never have imagined.

Alfred Greene

8

Chapter 1: The Price is Right... Or Is It?

The Dance of Supply and Demand

Picture two friends, Sarah and Mike, sitting at their favorite café, contemplating their caffeine cravings. As they browse the menu, they notice that the price of a latte has suddenly gone up by fifty cents. What's going on here? Did the barista just decide to keep an extra few cents for a rainy day? Or could there be something deeper, something that explains how prices move up and down in the marketplace?

At its heart, the relationship between supply and demand is the backbone of economics. It's the dance that determines how much we pay for our morning coffee, our cars, and even the latest smartphone. Supply is about how much of a good or service is available, while demand is about how much people want and can afford to buy. When we understand these ideas, we become better equipped to make smart choices with our money.

Let's go back to our café. If everyone suddenly wants lattes—maybe a new health trend is calling for more caffeine—while the supply stays the same, the price will likely go up. On the flip side, if a coffee roaster nearby has tons of beans and makes lots of lattes, the café might lower its prices to pull in more customers. This back-and-forth isn't just some academic exercise; it's the heartbeat of how markets operate.

To get a clearer picture of supply and demand, let's look at a few key terms. Equilibrium is that perfect point where the number of goods available matches what people want to buy. Think of it like a seesaw that's balanced just right—neither side is too heavy. When there's a surplus, it means there's more supply than demand, resulting in extra goods that sellers find hard to move. In our café example, this might mean too many pastries that, if unsold, could end up stale. On the other hand, a shortage happens when demand is greater than supply, leaving eager customers disappointed—imagine the chaos if the café runs out of its sought-after pumpkin spice lattes on a chilly autumn morning!

You might be wondering how this whole system works so smoothly, often without any noticeable bumps. That's where the concept of the "invisible hand" comes in, a term created by economist Adam Smith. It refers to the unseen forces that guide people's self-interested decisions, leading to outcomes that benefit society as a whole. Visualize a bustling marketplace where buyers and sellers, driven by their own needs and wants, come together to create a lively economy. The choices individuals make—what to buy, what to sell, and how much to charge—shape the market. This invisible hand helps ensure that resources flow effectively, adjusting to the ever-changing desires of consumers.

As we navigate these economic waters, it's important to understand that supply and demand aren't set in stone. They are flexible ideas affected by many factors—some easy to predict, others completely surprising. For example, think about how a sudden shortage of cocoa beans could jack up chocolate prices. If a terrible disease wipes out crops, there will be fewer beans to make chocolate. The supply curve shifts left, showing less availability. If people still crave chocolate, this increased demand will lead to higher prices at the store. Suddenly, that rich chocolate bar we used to buy without a second thought feels like a luxury.

It's also crucial to recognize that government actions can interfere with this natural balance. Price controls, taxes, and subsidies can have unintended effects. Imagine a government capping rent prices to help people afford housing. While the goal might be good, it can sometimes lead to fewer places to rent because landlords might pull out of the market or let their properties fall into disrepair. The very thing intended to help can sometimes end up hurting those it aims to support.

Understanding these principles is vital for making smart financial choices. Whether you're haggling over the price of a car, considering a job offer, or deciding how much to spend on dinner, supply and demand are always at play, quietly influencing your decisions. By seeing how prices change, you can navigate market dynamics more effectively and steer clear of potential problems.

Exploring supply and demand also sheds light on why consumers behave the way they do. Have you ever wondered why some tech gadgets fly off the shelves while others sit around gathering dust? When a new smartphone launches, demand often spikes because of the excitement surrounding the latest features. Older models, however, may struggle to find buyers, leading to price cuts to clear out inventory. Understanding these trends can help you time your purchases better, taking advantage of seasonal sales or product releases.

Moreover, the effects of supply and demand go beyond just individual decisions and reach into the larger economic picture. When we grasp these concepts, we become more aware of what influences financial markets, job availability, and even international trade. For instance, the rise of online shopping has shifted demand away from brick-and-mortar stores, pushing traditional retailers to adapt or risk becoming obsolete. Being able to spot these changes can give you a leg up in your personal and professional life.

As we delve deeper into the nuances of supply and demand, we'll uncover real-life examples that show these principles in action. From buzzing coffee shops to car dealerships trying to grab your attention, we'll see how these market dynamics shape our everyday experiences. More importantly, we'll reveal the stories behind the numbers, making these economic ideas relatable and easy to grasp.

In short, getting a handle on the dance of supply and demand is like having a map in a busy city. It gives you the information you need to navigate the complexities of the market, helping you make decisions that support your financial goals. As we continue to explore these principles, remember that economics isn't just for scholars or analysts; it's for everyone who wants to understand their financial world better. The interaction between supply and demand isn't just a dry theory; it's a living part of our daily lives that affects us all.

Everyday Examples: Insight from Coffee Shops to Car Dealerships

Imagine stepping into your favorite coffee shop, the warm aroma of fresh coffee wrapping around you like a hug. You glance at the menu, and your heart drops when you notice that your beloved latte now costs a bit more than it did last week. What's going on? Is the café owner just in a mood, or is something bigger happening? The reality is, your coffee shop is a small glimpse into the larger economic forces of supply and demand, where every price change has a story to tell about the market.

In the world of coffee, a lot of factors can affect both how much coffee people want and how much is available. First off, let's set the stage. Coffee demand usually stays pretty high; for many, a morning cup is non-negotiable, and café culture thrives in cities all over. But what if a coffee farm suffers a bad drought? Or think about how rising shipping costs from fluctuating fuel prices could mean fewer coffee beans make it to your favorite café. The barista isn't raising prices on a whim; they're reacting to real market conditions.

Now, let's turn our attention elsewhere: what happens if a fancy new coffee shop pops up nearby? Suddenly, there's competition, and that could change everything. Customers might rush over to check out unique flavors, artisanal brewing techniques, or a trendy vibe. This shift in demand might prompt your go-to café to lower prices or roll out special deals just to keep patrons walking through the door. This back-and-forth dance of demand and competition shows just how much businesses need to adapt to stay relevant.

This back-and-forth between competition and what customers want is especially clear during special events or seasonal changes. Take winter, for example. Everyone starts craving cozy, warm drinks, leading to a boost in demand for hot beverages. Cafés often take advantage of this by introducing seasonal flavors or limited-time specials like peppermint mochas. If the ingredients for those festive drinks become scarce, you can bet that your favorite café will adjust its prices. It's a balancing act of keeping customers happy while also making sure the business stays profitable.

Now, let's shift gears to something a bit larger and more intimidating: car dealerships. Buying a car can feel like a big deal—exciting, but also a bit nerve-wracking. When you walk onto the lot, you're met with rows of shiny vehicles, each with a price tag that might make your heart skip a beat. So why do prices fluctuate so much from one dealership to another or even among different models of the same brand?

The answer lies in supply and demand, mixed with some unique factors in the auto industry. For example, picture a new car model that has just hit the market and is causing a buzz. The demand for that model might skyrocket, thanks to ads bragging about the latest tech and performance. If the dealership has only a few of these sought-after cars, you guessed it—the prices might go up, making that car feel a bit more out of reach.

On the flip side, if a particular model isn't selling well—maybe because of bad reviews or another car stealing the spotlight—the dealership may have to cut prices to move that inventory. It's reasonable to expect promotional events or clearance sales as dealerships create a sense of urgency to sell those cars. If they notice that buyers are looking for a certain feature—like fuel efficiency during a spike in gas prices—they'll adjust their marketing and pricing to meet that demand.

Financing options are also a big player in the car buying game. The finance world is closely linked to supply and demand. When interest rates are low, more people are likely to finance a car, increasing demand. But if rates go up, potential buyers may hesitate, worrying about higher monthly payments.

Dealerships have to navigate this tricky landscape, adjusting their offers and financing packages to entice buyers. This often results in special deals that reflect the current state of the market.

Let's also consider how consumer perception impacts both coffee and cars. Branding can greatly influence how customers view products and prices. A well-known coffee chain might charge more for a cup, banking on its brand image and the quality people associate with it. Meanwhile, a lesser-known local café could serve a similar drink at a lower price, but it may take customers a while to feel comfortable making the switch.

Similarly, brand loyalty is a strong force in the car market. Many people stick with a particular car brand due to past experiences or family ties, often spending more for cars from that brand. The link between brand perception and pricing shows how psychological factors can mix with economic principles.

These concepts become even more complex when we think about seasonal trends and market swings that affect supply and demand in both industries. For instance, the car market often sees spikes in purchases during certain times of the year, like summer or holidays. Dealerships might ramp up their inventory in anticipation, only to find that unexpected events—like a pandemic—can completely change the game, leading to shortages or surpluses that impact prices.

It's clear that coffee shops and car dealerships give us valuable insights into the bigger picture of supply and demand. They remind us that our buying decisions aren't made in a vacuum. Every time you visit a café or a car dealership, you're influenced by countless factors—from changing consumer preferences to broader economic conditions. Every cup of coffee or new car is a choice shaped by a complex web of market forces.

The ripples from these everyday examples reach into larger economic discussions. As consumers, understanding how market dynamics impact our decisions can empower us to navigate our financial choices more effectively. For instance, recognizing when demand is high for a certain car model could help you negotiate a better price if you're willing to wait. Or being aware of supply issues in the coffee market might encourage you to try a new drink or brand, potentially leading to a delightful surprise.

We should also think about how technology is changing supply and demand in these areas. With more people ordering coffee online or researching cars, the way we buy things is evolving. The rise of delivery services has changed how coffee shops work, shifting supply and demand in new directions. Now, customers can have artisanal coffee brought right to their homes, creating fresh competition and pricing models in the market.

As we chew on these examples, it becomes clear that the principles of supply and demand are everywhere, guiding our choices in ways we might not even notice. From deciding between a quick caffeine fix or a leisurely coffee break to making the big decision to buy a new car, every choice is connected to the intricate dance of market dynamics. The stories that unfold in our daily experiences are a testament to the strong influence these economic forces have on all of us.

By tuning into the subtle signals around us, we can become more knowledgeable consumers, ready to make choices that align with our needs and financial goals. It goes beyond the price on a menu or a sticker on a car; it's about understanding what drives those costs and how they reflect the ongoing dance of supply and demand that shapes our economic landscape.

So, the next time you're savoring an overpriced latte or wandering a dealership lot, take a moment to appreciate the intricate ballet happening behind the scenes. Remember, you're not just a consumer; you're a vital piece of this economic puzzle, influencing and being influenced by the forces of supply, demand, and everything in between. Every choice you make can create ripples in the market, shaping the landscape for yourself and others, connecting us all in this intricate web of economic relationships.

The Invisible Hand: How Choices Shape the Market

Imagine walking into a grocery store. As you step inside, you are greeted by a burst of sensations: the bright colors of fresh fruits and vegetables, the warm, inviting smell of baked goods, and the lively chatter of shoppers filling their carts. You weave through aisles brimming with countless options, each product eager to catch your eye. While you make your selections, it's easy to forget just how much your choices affect the market as a whole.

Every time you decide what to buy—whether it's organic kale or regular lettuce, indulgent artisanal cheese or the less expensive store brand—you're playing a vital role in shaping the ever-changing dance of supply and demand. Although these choices might seem small and insignificant on their own, they contribute to a larger story that reflects consumer preferences, trends, and the ups and downs of the economy.

Take, for example, the growing popularity of plant-based diets. Over the last few years, more and more people have started choosing vegan and vegetarian options. What began as a niche market has burst into the mainstream, with grocery shelves now brimming with plant-based alternatives. This shift didn't just happen on its own; it shows a collective decision to focus on health, environmental sustainability, and animal welfare.

When consumers opt for plant-based products, they send a strong message to producers: these items are in demand. Companies, eager to profit from this trend, respond by increasing production, investing in new ideas, and refining their supply chains to keep up with this rising interest. This is where the concept of the "invisible hand," a term introduced by Adam Smith, comes into play. It suggests that resources will naturally move toward what people want, without any central authority telling them what to do.

The effects of your choices go far beyond just your local grocery store. As the demand for plant-based products rises, traditional meat and dairy industries feel the heat. Companies scramble to adapt, resulting in a ripple effect throughout the agricultural sector. Farmers might shift to growing more soybeans or almonds instead of raising cattle, thus changing the landscape of agriculture. Supply chains adapt, investments in new technologies grow, and the entire food production system evolves in reaction to what consumers want.

But it's not only individual choices that shape the market; outside factors also play a big role. For example, government rules and policies can help or hinder market dynamics. Take subsidies for electric vehicles, which are sparking a booming market for eco-friendly transportation. When the government encourages people to buy these cars, automakers feel the pressure to invest in research and development to create more models that fit this shift. The impact is significant: the automotive industry evolves, charging stations become more common, and consumers gain a wider range of options at various price points.

Technology also plays a huge part in changing supply and demand. Let's look at farming. Innovations like precision agriculture, which uses data and advanced machinery to maximize crop yields, have dramatically boosted production. Because of this, prices for certain goods may drop as they become more available, benefiting consumers while creating new challenges for farmers who are trying to maintain their profits. The balancing act of supply and demand is always shifting, adjusting to what consumers want, new technologies, and changes in regulations.

Let's dig into how these elements are all connected. Think about the rise of electric vehicles again. As more people become aware of climate change and the downsides of fossil fuels, many are choosing to invest in electric cars. This collective choice doesn't just affect the automotive industry; it also sparks changes in the energy sector. The increased demand for electric vehicles drives the need for renewable energy sources, leading to more investments in solar and wind technology. This transformation creates jobs, affects energy prices, and encourages innovation across different industries—a perfect example of how individual choices can have widespread consequences.

However, the market isn't just a straightforward system; it's a complex web of interactions that can lead to unexpected results. For instance, when a new smartphone model hits the market, it doesn't just change the phone industry; it also impacts many related sectors. Accessories like cases, chargers, and even app development boom as a result of the new phone's popularity. Here, choices made by consumers ripple through connected markets, highlighting the intricate relationships that make up our economy.

Consumer preferences can also be inconsistent and influenced by trends that come and go. Consider the recent boom in gluten-free products. With growing awareness of gluten sensitivity and celiac disease, consumers started flocking to gluten-free options. The market responded with a vast array of gluten-free snacks, baked goods, and even pasta. However, as people start to question the health benefits of gluten-free diets, demand might drop, leaving an excess of these products on the shelves. Once again, the invisible hand guides the market based on consumer interests, revealing both the power and unpredictability of choice.

As you navigate through your grocery shopping, take a moment to think about the larger impact of your selections. Every time you choose a local product over a mass-produced one, you're making a difference. Your demand for local goods encourages farmers and artisans to produce more, helping local economies and reducing environmental impact. Likewise, choosing fair-trade brands positively affects the lives of farmers and workers in developing countries, ensuring they receive fair compensation for their hard work. Each purchase acts as a vote, and every decision you make helps shape the direction of the market.

There's also a fascinating psychological side to consumer choice. Branding, marketing, and social influence can heavily sway decisions, often leading people to pay more for a product simply because of how it's perceived. Take the luxury goods market, for example, where the difference often lies not just in quality but also in brand prestige. Luxury brands thrive on the idea that high prices equal exclusivity and desirability, encouraging consumers to spend more than they might for similar quality elsewhere. This social dynamic illustrates how consumer perceptions and choices can shape entire market segments, affecting pricing strategies and production methods.

As we navigate through this complex world of choices and their effects, we must recognize the importance of making informed decisions. Consumers who understand how their choices impact the market are better equipped to make decisions that align with their values and financial goals. Being aware of market trends, technological advances, and regulatory changes allows consumers to be proactive rather than reactive when it comes to their spending.

To highlight this point, consider the recent surge in interest surrounding sustainable products. As consumers learn more about the environmental effects of their choices, many are opting for eco-friendly alternatives. From biodegradable packaging to companies that prioritize sustainability, the demand for green products is reshaping the market. Businesses that catch onto this trend and adapt their practices are likely to thrive, while those that ignore it may struggle to keep up.

The consumer is not just a passive player in this economic game; they are an active participant. Every choice made contributes to a larger narrative, influencing market dynamics in both obvious and subtle ways. This realization can feel empowering; knowing that your spending habits can boost certain industries and hold back others can change how you approach your purchases.

As we think about the connections between consumer choices and market outcomes, it's important to recognize the responsibility that comes with being a consumer. With each purchase, we hold the power to encourage ethical business practices, support local economies, and advocate for sustainable production methods. Our choices can drive change, pushing businesses to prioritize responsible practices and hold them accountable for their impact on society and the environment.

In summary, the invisible hand of the market is intricately linked with the choices we make every day. From the local coffee shop to the car dealership, our purchasing decisions ripple across industries, affecting everything from prices to production methods. As we become more thoughtful consumers, understanding the impact of our choices can lead to more mindful decisions—resulting in a market that better reflects our values and aspirations. Every time we reach for that item on the shelf, we're partaking in a grand economic dance, where our steps can influence the future of the marketplace.

So, the next time you find yourself in the grocery aisle or considering a big purchase, take a moment to think about the power of your choices. The invisible hand isn't some distant concept; it's actively at work in your everyday life, shaping not just the market but the broader economic story we all share. Every choice counts, and in this interconnected world, the waves created by our decisions can lead to significant changes in the marketplace for years to come.

Alfred Greene

28

Chapter 2: More Than a Dollar Store: How Businesses Set Prices

The Cost Puzzle: Factors Influencing Product Pricing

When you walk through the aisles of your local supermarket or browse the countless options online, have you ever wondered what really shapes the price of each product? Beyond the bright labels and enticing promotions lies a web of factors that influence how much you pay for that jar of organic peanut butter or that stylish new smartphone. Pricing isn't just about adding a certain percentage to the cost; it's a careful process shaped by production costs, competition, and market demand. Let's break down this cost puzzle together.

First up are production costs. Every product you see comes with its own set of costs that businesses have to consider when setting a price. These costs can be divided into two main types: fixed and variable. Fixed costs stay the same no matter how many items are produced, while variable costs can change based on production levels. For example, think of a toy manufacturer that makes colorful plastic figurines. Fixed costs might include rent for the factory, salaries for full-time workers, and depreciation on equipment. Whether the factory makes 1,000 or 10,000 toys, those costs don't change.

In contrast, the variable costs for that toy manufacturer cover things like raw materials, paint, and packaging—these can vary significantly depending on how many toys are made. If demand for the toys skyrockets and they need to produce more, the cost for raw materials will rise as well. It's crucial for businesses to understand the balance between fixed and variable costs to price their products correctly. If they get it wrong, they might end up losing money on each sale or pricing themselves out of the market.

Now, let's take a closer look at production costs, focusing on raw materials, labor, and overhead expenses. Raw materials can make up a large chunk of the total cost, especially in manufacturing. For instance, if the price of plastic goes up because of rising oil costs, the toy manufacturer will need to rethink their pricing strategy. Labor costs also play a big role; if there aren't enough skilled workers available, wages could increase, driving production costs higher.

Overhead expenses—like utilities, maintenance, and administrative costs—are also vital to pricing. If a company doesn't factor these expenses in, it could hurt their bottom line. Picture a bakery that makes artisanal bread. Along with the costs for flour and yeast, the bakery has to account for rent, utilities, and wages for bakers. All these elements come together to give a complete picture of production costs, which directly affects the final price you see on the shelf.

Next, let's talk about competition. The marketplace is a dynamic place where businesses compete for your attention, and pricing often acts as a key tactic in this battle. It's important to be aware of what competitors are charging. Imagine you own a local coffee shop. If your competitor charges $3 for a cappuccino, you'll need to think about how this impacts your pricing. Should you match their price, or should you offer something special to justify a higher one?

Sometimes, businesses get caught up in "price wars," where they continuously lower prices to attract more customers. Think about those supermarket chains that often run eye-catching promotions. They might sell certain items at a loss to draw people in, hoping that once customers arrive, they will also buy other products to make up for the loss. This competitive environment can change quickly, making pricing a constant challenge.

Additionally, businesses can adopt different pricing strategies like penetration pricing or skimming. Penetration pricing means setting a low initial price to get customers on board and gain market share, while skimming involves starting with a high price and gradually lowering it as the product becomes more popular. Each strategy has its own risks and rewards, and the most successful companies know how to adjust their pricing as needed.

Let's also look at market demand, the classic concept of supply and demand that influences every sale. When people really want a product, they're often willing to pay more for it. On the flip side, when demand drops, prices usually fall. You can see this in action with gasoline prices, which can change dramatically based on the time of year. During summer vacation, when families are traveling, gas prices tend to rise. In winter, however, demand decreases, and prices typically drop as companies try to sell off their inventory.

But it's not just about demand and supply; it's also about how sensitive consumers are to price changes, which is known as elasticity. Luxury items, like designer handbags, often have elastic demand. A small price increase can lead to a big drop in sales. On the other hand, necessities like bread tend to have inelastic demand; people will buy it even if the price goes up because they need it.

Let's see how elasticity affects pricing strategies. A beverage company launching a new soda flavor might kick things off with a low price of just 99 cents to get customers to try it. If the price is too high and demand slips, they may need to quickly change their strategy to avoid having too much stock. Conversely, if the new flavor is a hit, they might gradually increase the price while still keeping it within reach.

To show how demand can drive prices, think about limited-time offers. When something is scarce, it often makes people want it even more. Take a popular fast-food chain that introduces a limited-time burger. Fans will likely rush to the restaurants, allowing the company to charge a higher price knowing that interest will outstrip supply during that promotion.

In summary, setting a price for a product is a complex task that requires a solid understanding of various factors like production costs, competition, and consumer demand. Companies must carefully navigate this intricate puzzle to find prices that cover their costs while drawing in customers and maximizing profits. So, the next time you reach for your wallet, think about all the different elements that have influenced that price tag. There's a lot of economic thought behind it—much more than you might expect!

Understanding Profit Margins: Pricing Strategies Explained

Entering the world of business is like stepping onto a dance floor. It requires not just a sense of rhythm but also a deep understanding of the intricacies involved in making a profit. At the center of this dance is the idea of profit margins. Profit margins are the heartbeat of any business; they determine not only survival but also growth and sustainability. As we explore different pricing strategies, we'll uncover how these approaches affect profit margins and, ultimately, the success of a business.

Let's begin with one of the simplest ways to set a price: cost-plus pricing. Picture a charming little bakery, filled with the delightful scent of freshly baked treats. Imagine the skilled baker measuring out flour, sugar, and eggs, with each ingredient playing a crucial role in creating a scrumptious cupcake. The bakery owner, eager to keep the business running, needs to figure out how much to charge for that cupcake. This is where cost-plus pricing comes in. It's as straightforward as it sounds: add a set markup to the total cost of making the product.

In our bakery example, the cost of a cupcake includes the ingredients and labor.

Let's say the total comes to $1 for one cupcake. The owner might decide to add a 50% markup. So, the price would be calculated like this: $1 (cost) + $0.50 (markup) = $1.50. This method is not only easy to understand but also guarantees that the bakery covers its expenses while enjoying a profit margin of 33% for every cupcake sold.

Cost-plus pricing is popular, especially among small businesses and manufacturers, because it's simple and effective. However, it does have its downsides. For one, it doesn't consider what customers are willing to pay or the demand in the market. If our bakery finds out that a nearby shop sells similar cupcakes for $2, they might need to rethink their pricing strategy. Just adding a markup might not be enough to attract customers. So, while cost-plus pricing is a reasonable starting point, it's important to understand its limitations in a competitive market.

Now, let's explore a more nuanced method—value-based pricing. With this strategy, the focus shifts from production costs to how much consumers believe the product is worth. Think about an Apple store, bustling with customers excited to buy the latest iPhone. Apple has perfected value-based pricing by creating a brand that stands for innovation and quality. People are willing to spend more on an iPhone not just because of its features but also because of the status and identity that comes with owning one.

Value-based pricing starts with understanding what customers find valuable. Companies using this approach conduct thorough market research to discover what consumers truly appreciate. This might involve surveys, focus groups, or looking at buying trends—all aimed at establishing a perceived value that goes beyond the actual production cost. For example, if Apple knows that their customers associate their phones with cutting-edge technology, they can set higher prices that match that perception.

Take a look at luxury brands like Louis Vuitton and Rolex. They don't just sell products; they offer an experience, a lifestyle, and a sense of identity. A handbag or a watch isn't merely a functional item; it's a statement. By creating this perceived value, these brands can charge premium prices while maintaining strong profit margins. On the other hand, a company that only focuses on production costs may struggle to compete with a brand that effectively communicates its unique value.

In the world of value-based pricing, success relies on staying connected with customers and adapting to their changing perceptions and desires. Companies need to ask themselves questions like: What do our customers truly value? How can we enhance that value? This ongoing conversation helps businesses adjust their pricing strategies while maximizing profit margins.

Next up is a modern concept that has transformed the pricing game: dynamic pricing. This approach involves changing prices in real-time based on several factors, like demand, competition, and even the time of day. Industries such as airlines and hospitality have embraced dynamic pricing to boost profits and manage their inventory efficiently.

Imagine booking a flight on a popular airline. You might notice that ticket prices can change drastically from one moment to the next. This is thanks to sophisticated algorithms that analyze data—everything from ticket sales to competitor prices and seasonal trends. If a flight is filling up quickly, the airline may raise prices to take advantage of the demand. Conversely, if a flight isn't booking well, prices might drop to attract more travelers.

Let's consider a case study involving a major airline. During busy travel times, like summer vacations or holidays, ticket prices often soar. The airline knows that families are willing to pay more during these periods to secure their travel. In contrast, during quieter times when fewer people are flying, the same airline might offer big discounts to draw in customers. This strategic use of dynamic pricing helps maximize revenue while keeping profit margins healthy throughout the year.

However, dynamic pricing isn't without its challenges. It can frustrate consumers who feel like they're being played when prices change. Transparency is key here; customers appreciate knowing why prices fluctuate. If an airline is open about its pricing model, it can build trust and loyalty, even when costs vary.

As we look at these different pricing strategies, it becomes clear that understanding profit margins is vital for making smart pricing decisions. Cost-plus pricing provides a basic foundation, while value-based pricing puts the spotlight on what consumers think matters. Dynamic pricing, meanwhile, adds flexibility that can really benefit businesses.

In the end, the interaction of these strategies shows how complex pricing can be in today's market. Each method has its own set of opportunities and challenges, but they all share the common goal of maximizing profits while delivering value to customers. For business owners, the trick is to recognize the strengths and weaknesses of each approach and adapt them to fit their market conditions.

No matter which strategy is chosen, the importance of profit margins remains a constant in this ever-changing landscape. As businesses strive to find the right price point, they should remember that pricing isn't just a figure; it reflects their brand, values, and understanding of customer behavior. In a world where consumers have endless choices at their fingertips, those who master the art of pricing will stand out from the crowd.

So, the next time you come across a price tag, take a moment to think about all the factors that influenced that number. From the straightforward calculations of a local bakery to the complex algorithms of major airlines, pricing strategies play a role in our daily lives, shaping how we shop, travel, and experience the world. Understanding these strategies can empower you as a consumer and as a knowledgeable participant in the vibrant world of commerce.

Price Psychology: Crafting Attractive Prices for Consumers

When we explore how people make choices about buying things, we uncover a fascinating reality: prices are not just dull numbers that tell us how much we need to pay for items. Instead, they are deeply connected to the way we think and feel about what we buy. As we look into the world of price psychology, we discover the clever techniques businesses use to guide our shopping habits and influence how we view value.

Let's start with charm pricing, a well-known strategy in retail. Have you ever noticed something priced at $9.99 instead of a nice, round $10.00? That's charm pricing at work! While it might seem like a small detail, it reveals a lot about how our minds work. Studies show that we tend to see prices ending in ".99" as being much lower than the rounded prices, even if there's only a one-cent difference. It's an interesting quirk; we focus on the first digit, and prices like $9.99 feel like great deals, while $10.00 can seem like a big expense.

Think about your own shopping experiences. When you see a price tag of $9.99, does it catch your eye more than a $10.00 tag? For many people, the answer is a clear yes. Behavioral economists have dug deep into this idea and found that the leftmost digit has a strong impact on our thinking. Since we read numbers from left to right, a price like $9.99 suggests a much lower cost compared to $10.00, even though the difference is tiny.

In real life, charm pricing can make a big difference in sales. Retailers and marketers know how to use it to spark impulse buys. Picture this: you walk into a store, browsing around, and spot a lovely dress priced at $49.99 instead of $50.00. That one cent may not seem like much, but it creates a feeling of getting a great bargain. This is why charm pricing is used everywhere—from clothing shops to grocery stores—each using this technique to grab your attention and boost sales.

But charm pricing isn't the only trick in the book. Another interesting method is called anchoring. Anchoring is when we lean too much on the first piece of information we see when making decisions. In terms of pricing, our first encounter with a price can greatly influence how we see the prices that come after it.

Imagine walking into an electronics store and spotting a shiny new TV priced at $2,000. Next to it, there's a similar model marked at $1,500. Suddenly, the second one looks like an amazing deal, even if it's still more than you wanted to spend. That's anchoring in action. The first price of $2,000 sets the stage, making the second price look more appealing just by comparison.

Retailers know this psychological trick well and often use it cleverly. Think of the classic "compare at" price. When you see a label that says "originally $500, now $350," your mind quickly jumps to calculate how much you're saving. The anchoring effect makes the discounted price even more attractive, nudging you toward a purchase you might not have considered otherwise. It creates excitement and urgency, allowing many to feel they are snatching up a fantastic deal.

This approach isn't just for brick-and-mortar stores. Online shops often use similar methods, showing a higher price crossed out next to a sale price. This visual difference enhances the idea of value, making the lower price hard to resist. Thanks to anchoring, what might have been a hesitant decision to buy can quickly turn into an impulsive click of the "buy now" button.

As we dig deeper into price psychology, we also come across the ideas of scarcity and urgency—the powerful forces that push consumers to make quick decisions. Businesses have long known how effective limited-time offers and exclusive deals can be in creating urgency. When people see a product as hard to find, their desire for it grows, often leading them to buy on impulse.

Think about flash sales or limited-edition releases. When a popular sneaker brand announces a limited drop of a highly sought-after model, the excitement is almost tangible. The combination of scarcity—only a handful of pairs available—and urgency— available for just a short time—creates a buzz that prompts customers to act quickly before they miss out. This is especially true in streetwear, where brand collaborations lead to releases that sell out in just minutes.

Let's look at a case study involving a well-known sneaker brand. When they shared news of a limited-release sneaker online, the excitement was immense. The pre-launch marketing gave consumers sneak peeks of the product, but the catch was clear: only a limited number of pairs would be made available. On launch day, devoted fans, sneaker enthusiasts, and casual buyers rushed to the website, eager to click "add to cart" and grab their pair.

In this world of scarcity and urgency, FOMO—the fear of missing out—plays a major role. People feel driven by the worry of being left out, pushing them to make choices they might hesitate on in other situations. This fear can be a strong motivator for purchases, making shoppers feel like they have to act fast or risk losing something special.

However, the genius of these strategies isn't just in their ability to inspire quick purchases; they also shape how consumers behave in the long run. When shoppers frequently encounter charm pricing, anchoring, and time-sensitive offers, they start to expect these tactics in their shopping experiences. Over time, this can lead consumers to become more impulsive, often choosing perceived deals over thoughtful buying decisions.

Exploring the world of price psychology shows us how businesses skillfully tap into our mental shortcuts and emotional triggers. Prices aren't just plain numbers; they are carefully designed signals meant to attract our attention and sway our choices. As we examine these strategies—charm pricing, anchoring, and scarcity—we gain a deeper understanding of what influences our buying behavior.

So, the next time you find yourself drawn to a price that seems like an incredible deal, or feel the push to grab something because of a limited-time offer, take a moment to think about how your choices are being influenced. Understanding the psychology behind pricing not only empowers you as a shopper but also gives you the tools to navigate the complex world of shopping. By recognizing these strategies, you can make smarter choices—balancing what you want with a clearer understanding of what's truly valuable.

In the end, the interaction of price psychology offers us a glimpse into the larger economic picture. As consumers, we have the power to interpret these signals and respond in ways that reflect our personal values and goals. The next time you look at a price tag, remember that behind those numbers lies a rich world of psychological insights, designed to make you rethink what you value and how much you're willing to pay. By understanding these pricing tricks, you can shop more mindfully, turning you into a savvy consumer who can skillfully navigate the complexities of today's marketplace.

Alfred Greene

46

Chapter 3: When Shelves Go Bare: Understanding Supply Shortages

Analyzing Recent Shortages: Case Studies and Lessons

To truly understand the impact of supply shortages, we need to reflect on some striking examples that shook our consumer society to its core. These events didn't just cause market disruptions; they changed how we view supply chains, consumer habits, and even our everyday lives. What we once took for granted—like a simple roll of toilet paper—became a sought-after item, leading to odd behaviors and a frantic urgency. By looking at these case studies, we can grasp not only the complexities of supply and demand but also prepare ourselves for the surprises that come with living in such an interconnected world.

Let's dive into the notorious toilet paper shortage during the COVID-19 pandemic. It's hard to forget the bizarre scenes in grocery stores where shelves that used to be fully stocked with toilet paper were suddenly bare. Panic buying took over as people rushed to hoard essential goods, especially toilet paper, resulting in empty aisles and a cultural moment we never thought we'd witness. You might remember the chaos: shoppers jostling for position, their carts overflowing with rolls of toilet paper, creating makeshift barricades. This behavior wasn't just a quirky reaction; it was driven by fear and a sense of scarcity, pushing consumers into survival mode.

So, what sparked this mad rush? To get to the bottom of the toilet paper shortage, we first need to understand how it's made and distributed. Unlike many products that come in various types and sizes, toilet paper is typically produced in a few large factories that operate on set schedules, producing specific amounts to keep things efficient. But when the pandemic struck and lockdowns were enforced, the demand for toilet paper shot up. With people staying at home more than ever, no one wanted to find themselves without this basic necessity during a global health crisis.

Even though demand was soaring, the supply chain couldn't keep up. The toilet paper industry faced an unexpected spike that overwhelmed their production capabilities. Transport routes were disrupted due to lockdown measures, and with everyone hoarding supplies, even the best-prepared companies saw their stock dwindle quickly. As consumers rushed to fill their carts, stores struggled to restock, creating a cycle of panic. This situation teaches us a key lesson about supply dynamics: even minor disruptions can lead to major shortages when fear drives consumers to act irrationally.

Another clear example of how fragile supply chains can be is the shortage of semiconductor chips, which are crucial in our tech-driven world. These tiny but powerful components are found in almost every modern device, from smartphones and laptops to household gadgets and, most importantly, cars. As car manufacturers ramped up production in the years leading to the pandemic, they became heavily reliant on these chips, often underestimating their vulnerability to disruptions. The COVID-19 pandemic revealed just how tight the margins were and highlighted how interconnected different sectors truly are.

The automotive industry found itself in a tight spot as the pandemic disrupted supply lines and forced factories to shut down. In response, chip manufacturers shifted their production to keep up with the demand for consumer electronics like computers and gaming consoles, as remote work and online gaming surged. Automakers suddenly realized they had made a risky bet on a single, fragile supply chain. The outcome? A shortage that halted production, delayed vehicle deliveries, and ultimately pushed prices higher for consumers.

The semiconductor shortage showcases another important aspect of supply and demand: the ripple effect. This economic concept explains how one shortage can lead to a chain reaction of shortages across different industries. As car production slowed, the availability of vehicles decreased, driving prices up even further. The once-stable automotive market saw wild fluctuations, leaving consumers with fewer choices and higher costs. It's a striking reminder that in a global economy, the troubles of one sector can have far-reaching effects.

In both the toilet paper and semiconductor chip situations, we not only witness the immediate impacts of supply shortages but also the long-term changes they can bring about in consumer behavior and business practices. Panic buying became a common sight during the pandemic as people realized that supply could no longer be taken for granted. On the flip side, companies started reevaluating their supply chain strategies, recognizing the importance of being flexible and diverse to handle unforeseen challenges.

A key takeaway from these case studies is the need for resilience when facing supply chain issues. Businesses should develop strategies that allow them to adapt quickly when the unexpected happens. For example, some companies began stockpiling essential components, anticipating possible shortages. Others adjusted their manufacturing processes to meet shifting demands, illustrating that being agile can be a lifesaver during tough times.

As we work through these challenges together, it becomes clear that they go beyond mere inconveniences. They reveal how delicate the balance between supply and demand can be and just how easily it can be disrupted. The lessons learned from these real-world examples provide valuable insights into the fragility of our systems and highlight the need for proactive strategies to ensure we're better prepared to tackle future challenges.

The Ripple Effect: Interconnections Across Industries

In a world where technology connects us faster than ever, it's surprising how vulnerable we still are to disruptions. Imagine the economy as a big orchestra, where each industry plays its unique role. When one instrument goes out of tune, the whole performance can fall apart. Shortages in one area send waves that ripple far beyond their immediate impact, revealing the intricate network of our global supply chain. These effects aren't just abstract concepts; they show up in real ways that affect prices, availability of goods, and trust among consumers.

Let's take copper as an example. This often-overlooked metal plays a crucial role in many applications, from electrical wiring to plumbing and even renewable energy technologies. When a shortage occurs in the copper market—perhaps due to mining strikes or geopolitical issues—it doesn't just hit the electrical industry. As copper prices rise, manufacturers in many areas suddenly see their costs skyrocket. This isn't just a minor hiccup; it flows down to consumers, leading to higher prices for electronics like laptops and smartphones. A single disruption in one sector can create a domino effect, impacting seemingly unrelated markets and ultimately tightening the financial grip on consumers.

To really get a sense of this interconnectedness, let's look at the automotive industry, which offers a clear example through the recent shortage of semiconductor chips. The pandemic changed consumer behavior dramatically, leading to a sudden drop in demand for personal vehicles as people shifted to remote work. Car manufacturers cut production, but when the world started to reopen, demand for cars surged again. Meanwhile, the semiconductor industry, which had shifted its focus to meet the growing demand for consumer electronics, found it couldn't keep up with the automotive sector's needs. The outcome? A ripple effect that disrupted multiple industries.

Automakers weren't the only ones affected. Steel producers, who provide essential materials for car manufacturing, faced a sharp drop in orders. With fewer cars being assembled, the demand for steel dipped, causing its prices to fluctuate as well. This decline rippled out further, affecting glass manufacturers who supply windshields and windows. As car production slowed down, the entire ecosystem that supports vehicle manufacturing had to adjust, forcing related industries to rethink their output and pricing strategies, leaving suppliers—and consumers—scrambling to keep up.

The pandemic served as a wake-up call, revealing just how interconnected our global supply chains really are. Natural disasters, political strife, and economic shifts in one region can shake supply chains all the way across the globe. For example, if a semiconductor factory in Taiwan is hit by a disaster, the effects can be felt in the automotive industry far away in Detroit. This highlights not only the vulnerability of supply lines but also how much entire sectors depend on the smooth functioning of these global networks.

In this web of connections, pricing becomes a fascinating topic to explore. As shortages ripple through the economy, we often see the emergence of inflation. With fewer supplies available, companies are pushed to raise their prices to maintain their profit margins. This isn't just about the cost of goods; it can lead to broader inflation in related sectors. For instance, if the price of a new car skyrockets because of chip shortages, it can drive up prices in the used car market as consumers look for alternatives.

Think about this: when a specific product becomes scarce, it doesn't just raise its price; it can also change how consumers behave. When people hear there's a shortage, they may panic-buy, which only worsens the situation. This was clearly seen during the pandemic when even rumors of toilet paper shortages sent shoppers into a frenzy. The psychology behind scarcity can unpredictably drive demand, making a product's value depend not just on its actual availability but also on how consumers feel about it.

As we consider how connected industries are, it becomes clear that businesses need to take a broader view of their supply chain strategies. The old way of relying on a single supplier is becoming riskier. Companies that once depended on a narrow range of suppliers are now realizing the importance of diversifying their sources for critical components. Some businesses have even started stockpiling essential materials like semiconductors and raw materials to prepare for potential future shortages. Others are investing in technology to improve visibility in their supply chains, using data analytics and machine learning to better predict demand and respond flexibly.

Innovation is also key to navigating the challenges of interconnected industries. As shortages arise, companies are forced to rethink their business models. For example, car manufacturers are exploring alternative materials for parts usually made with scarce resources. Electric vehicle makers, who often rely on rare minerals for battery production, are investing in recycling technologies to reclaim valuable materials instead of depending solely on new mining. These changes not only help address immediate shortages but also lay the groundwork for more sustainable practices in the long run.

Understanding the ripple effects across industries is crucial for consumers, businesses, and policymakers alike. When we recognize that our buying choices and production methods are part of a larger ecosystem, we can work towards being more resilient in the face of disruptions. By appreciating the complex dance of supply and demand, we can aim for a future that is both sustainable and interconnected.

As we navigate this intricate landscape, it's vital to stay alert and adaptable. Shortages are more than just inconveniences; they remind us of how fragile our systems can be and the ripple effects that can stem from seemingly isolated issues. Moving forward, the lessons learned from our interconnectedness will guide us toward a stronger and more resilient global economy, where the harmony of our economic orchestra can withstand the inevitable off-key notes that life throws our way.

Reacting to Scarcity: Consumer and Business Adaptations

In a world where supply chains usually run like a well-oiled machine, even a small hiccup can throw everything off balance. Shortages reveal just how fragile our interconnected systems can be, but they also ignite incredible creativity and adaptability, both in consumers and businesses. By looking at the strategies people and companies use to navigate these tough times, we can gain valuable insights into human behavior and corporate innovation when resources run low.

Let's start by examining how consumers adjust when faced with scarcity. People are naturally resourceful. When something becomes hard to find, shoppers often look for substitutes. Imagine walking into a store to find the toilet paper shelves completely empty, causing a wave of panic among shoppers. What's the solution? Suddenly, paper towels become a perfectly acceptable alternative. This change in consumer behavior highlights a broader trend: when faced with shortages, folks instinctively seek out alternatives that help them feel a little more normal. The psychology behind these choices is both fascinating and complex.

The habit of substituting products comes from a mix of necessity and creativity. When consumers encounter an empty shelf, their minds kick into high gear, searching for solutions. It's not just about the missing item; it's about finding a way to meet the underlying need that product once fulfilled. Toilet paper might be unavailable, but the need for cleanliness remains. In these moments, the ability to think on their feet can lead to surprising solutions. The same idea applies to other goods. When baking supplies ran low during the pandemic, clever home cooks found creative alternatives in their kitchens, whipping up treats with whatever ingredients they had.

Adaptability goes beyond just swapping products; it also shows up in the way people shop. Bulk-buying is a perfect example of this behavior. When people perceive scarcity, they often stock up on goods, which can lead to panic buying. This behavior is tied to the need for security; when running out of essentials feels imminent, it's only natural to create a safety net. However, this instinct can make shortages worse, creating a tricky situation during times of scarcity. Retailers, facing dwindling stock, find themselves caught in a loop where the more people panic-buy, the more real shortages occur.

The impact of these consumer adaptations reaches far beyond individual homes. As buying patterns shift, the dynamics of demand and supply change too. The marketplace becomes like a stage where consumers play a key role in shaping outcomes. In response to rising demand for alternative products, retailers often need to adjust their inventory strategies. The effects of consumer behavior ripple throughout the supply chain, influencing how goods move from producers to shoppers.

Now, let's turn our attention to businesses and see how they adapt. Just as individuals have learned to pivot, companies have also come up with strategies to handle supply shortages. One common approach is diversifying suppliers. Instead of depending on just one source for raw materials or parts, businesses are increasingly realizing the value of building a network of suppliers. This shift not only reduces risk but also boosts resilience. If one supplier runs into trouble, other options are available, allowing production to continue smoothly.

Moreover, companies are now more inclined to invest in technology to optimize their supply chains. This might involve using data analytics to predict demand trends or employing machine learning to make production processes more efficient. By embracing technology, businesses can make smarter decisions, enabling them to respond quickly to changing market conditions. This tech-savvy approach shows just how powerful innovation can be in navigating scarcity.

Take, for example, food manufacturers during the pandemic. When grain shortages hit due to disrupted logistics, many companies began experimenting with new ingredients or even switching gears to create different products altogether. This kind of innovation is crucial during tough times, as businesses need to be willing to think outside the box and explore new possibilities. The ability to pivot not only helps companies weather the storm but can also open up entirely new revenue streams.

Creativity doesn't stop there; it also extends to product design. When specific materials become scarce, businesses must adapt their offerings. Manufacturers of kitchen appliances, for instance, may find themselves unable to source certain components, pushing them to seek alternative materials or redesign their products entirely. This knack for innovation can transform a challenge into an opportunity, setting the stage for lasting changes in what's available and what consumers prefer.

As we dive into the strategies used by both consumers and businesses, we should also think about how these insights empower individuals. Understanding the economy is a crucial skill for navigating a world where supply and demand can change unexpectedly. Knowing how scarcity works helps consumers make better purchasing choices, encouraging them to seek alternatives or support local businesses during tough times. Equipped with this knowledge, individuals can actively engage in the marketplace instead of just reacting to its ups and downs.

Being mindful of shopping habits helps people understand market dynamics better. When consumers take a moment to think about what they really need versus what they want, they can make choices that align more closely with their values and situations. This might mean opting for a less popular brand or choosing second-hand items when new products are hard to come by. Every purchasing decision can become a conscious choice, reflecting a desire to adapt and be resilient in the face of economic uncertainty.

Additionally, consumers are encouraged to stay informed about market trends. By keeping an eye on industry news and emerging alternatives, individuals can anticipate potential shortages and adjust their shopping strategies. For instance, understanding the seasonal nature of some products can help them make smarter buying decisions throughout the year. With insights into how supply chains work, consumers can navigate scarcity with confidence.

As we reflect on the adaptive strategies used by consumers and businesses during shortages, it's clear that resilience is built on creativity and knowledge. The challenges that come with scarcity can spark amazing solutions, leading to resourceful and strategic shifts in behavior.

The connection between how consumers adapt and how businesses innovate paints a compelling picture of the need for flexibility in the economy. In uncertain times, both consumers and companies can adjust their responses, creating a more resilient and agile economic landscape. This spirit of adaptability not only helps us cope with immediate challenges but also lays the foundation for a sustainable future, where the lessons learned from scarcity shape our decisions moving forward.

Ultimately, navigating scarcity is about more than just getting by; it's about thriving. It's about recognizing the potential in every challenge and seizing the opportunities that come from adversity. By embracing adaptability and nurturing a proactive mindset, both individuals and businesses can emerge stronger, equipped to face whatever uncertainties lie ahead.

Chapter 4: Bargain Hunters and Luxury Lovers: The Power of Consumer Demand

Needs vs. Wants: Consumer Behavior and Market Influence

Understanding the difference between needs and wants is key to grasping how consumers behave, which in turn shapes our purchasing decisions and influences the market. At first glance, this distinction might seem straightforward, but as we dig deeper into what drives human desire and necessity, we realize that things can get a bit complicated. Needs are the essentials we cannot live without—things like food, water, and shelter—while wants are those things we crave for comfort, luxury, or to express ourselves.

Think about our most basic needs: food, water, and a place to live. These are the foundations of our survival. For instance, a family needs basic groceries like rice, vegetables, fruits, and proteins. These items are must-haves; without them, life cannot be sustained. On the flip side, the desire to enjoy a fancy coffee from a trendy café or to cruise around in a luxury car shows the other side of the coin. Sure, we can get by with just the essentials from the grocery store, but the appeal of a high-end coffee or a stylish car speaks to our aspirations, tastes, and social image.

The relationship between needs and wants gets even more interesting when we consider how culture affects our views. In many parts of the world, having clean water is a critical need, but in cities where tap water is readily available, bottled water has become a wanted item that many are happy to buy. Isn't it ironic? A basic necessity has been transformed into something fancy and desirable, often sold with an eye-catching label and a price that might make our ancestors shake their heads.

To add another layer to our conversation, let's look at Maslow's Hierarchy of Needs. This psychological theory breaks down human motivation into a five-level pyramid. At the bottom are our basic physiological needs—think food, water, warmth, and rest. As we go up the pyramid, we encounter safety needs, love and belonging, esteem, and finally, self-actualization at the top. This hierarchy offers valuable insights into why consumers make the choices they do. For example, if someone is struggling to meet their basic needs, they're not likely to be shopping for luxury items like the latest gadgets or designer clothes. On the other hand, someone who feels secure and fulfilled may be more inclined to indulge in their wants, looking for products that reflect their self-image or dreams.

Businesses know how important these psychological factors are and use them in their marketing strategies. Market segmentation is a big part of this. Companies divide consumers into groups based on things like demographics, lifestyles, and buying habits, so they can create marketing messages that really hit home. Imagine a campaign targeting young professionals, where the focus is on trendy office attire being framed as not just a want but a necessity for getting ahead in their careers. This turns a simple fashion choice into something that feels essential for success.

A great example of how needs and wants can shift is the rise of bottled water as a new necessity in urban areas. Not long ago, people filled their reusable containers from the tap; now, buying bottled water is a common practice, even celebrated by some as a lifestyle choice. Brands like Evian and Fiji have captured consumers' attention by marketing their water as an experience or even a status symbol. The message is clear: staying hydrated is important, but why not do it with a little flair?

As we explore the world of consumer demand, it's becoming clearer that businesses are not just selling products; they are reshaping what we think of as needs and wants. The trend of health-conscious marketing, for example, has led many to see organic produce not just as a luxury but as crucial for a healthy lifestyle. This trend shows how businesses can influence how we perceive our needs, impacting what we buy based on our desires to feel better and live healthier.

Additionally, as society changes, so do our definitions of needs and wants. Lately, sustainability has become a hot topic, leading many to view eco-friendly products as essential. What used to be a nice option—like buying reusable shopping bags or environmentally friendly cleaning supplies—has now turned into a moral choice for many shoppers. This shift demonstrates that consumer behavior is always in motion, changing with cultural trends and societal values.

By examining consumer behavior through the lens of needs and wants, we reveal a lively landscape where motivations meet market forces. This understanding helps consumers make smarter choices while encouraging businesses to adapt to changing desires. The impact of these ideas goes beyond just buying and selling; they shape how we view our lives, the roles we play in society, and the values we hold dear.

As we navigate the complexities of consumer demand, the relationship between psychological motivations, cultural influences, and market segmentation becomes even more important. The ongoing interaction between needs and wants not only influences individual choices but also weaves into the very fabric of the marketplace, highlighting the deep connections between human desires and economic realities.

Trend Setters: Social Factors Driving Demand

In the lively world of shopping, social factors have become a key player in what we decide to buy. As our daily lives mix with what's available in stores, our choices reflect not just our personal tastes but also the powerful impact of social media, community interactions, and cultural trends. The way we shop has turned into a complex dance of societal influences that shape our wants, motivations, and ultimately, our spending.

Social media influencers, those skilled storytellers of the digital age, are a major force in this changing landscape. With their thoughtfully designed feeds and engaging posts, they have the ability to set trends and influence lifestyles. Traditional advertising alone just doesn't cut it anymore; platforms like Instagram, TikTok, and YouTube have created a space where influencers tell stories about products that really connect with their followers. A single outfit post or morning routine video can spark a rush of interest for the items showcased, whether it's a skincare product, a trendy accessory, or the latest gadget. Influencers have turned promoting products into an art, crafting a sense of connection that older advertisements often miss.

Take fashion influencers, for example. They display their outfits and style choices, turning their everyday lives into a showcase for brands. Their followers, eager to mirror the lifestyles they see, are more likely to buy the same clothes, accessories, or beauty products featured in their posts. This has made influencers the trendsetters of our time, reshaping what's considered desirable and significantly boosting consumer demand.

Yet, it's not only about influencers; peer pressure and community connections also play a big role in how we shop. A great example can be found in youth culture, where trends can take off like wildfire in schools and social groups. The need to fit in and be accepted often drives individuals to seek out the latest fashions or gadgets that their friends deem "cool." Brands that present themselves as desirable in these social contexts often find themselves in the spotlight of consumer demand. This creates a cycle where social acceptance fuels excitement around certain products, making them even more popular.

You can see this blend of social influence and consumer choices in the rise of luxury brands, which thrive on the aspirational nature of their products. When a celebrity or influencer is spotted with a designer handbag, the demand for that item soars. It's clear that owning these products is not just about the items themselves; it's about the status they bring. Social media amplifies this, as pictures of luxury items are shared and admired, creating an almost overwhelming desire among followers to join in on the lifestyle being showcased.

However, it's crucial to realize that trends are always shifting; they're influenced by changes in culture. In recent years, there's been a strong movement toward sustainability and ethical consumption. More and more, consumers want products that match their values. This shift has changed the game, with eco-friendly brands gaining popularity as awareness of environmental issues grows. Shoppers don't just want to buy things anymore; they want their purchases to show a commitment to social responsibility.

For instance, the rise in popularity of vintage fashion is a great case in point. Items that were once considered secondhand or outdated have been reimagined as stylish and desirable, thanks in part to influencers showcasing thrifted finds online. Vintage fashion appeals to consumers for two main reasons: it allows them to express their unique style while supporting sustainability by giving new life to previously loved items. This trend speaks not only to personal taste but also aligns with a broader cultural move toward mindful buying.

Cultural movements like minimalism and ethical consumerism have also reshaped how we understand demand. Minimalism, which emphasizes simplicity and living intentionally, has encouraged many to rethink the need for excessive buying. As a result, brands that promote simple designs and sustainable practices are finding a welcoming audience. Consumers increasingly gravitate toward products that prioritize quality over quantity, reflecting a deeper desire for authenticity and purpose in their choices.

There are plenty of real-world examples of brands successfully navigating these social and cultural currents. Take Patagonia, for instance, which has built a strong reputation around environmental care. The company has tapped into the growing demand for sustainability, and its commitment to ethical practices, combined with engaging social media strategies, has made it a leader in the eco-friendly market. When consumers buy a jacket or outdoor gear from Patagonia, they're not just making a purchase; they're making a statement about their values.

Another notable example is Toms Shoes, which popularized the "one for one" business model. For every pair of shoes sold, they donate a pair to a child in need. This approach resonated with socially conscious shoppers who want to make a positive difference with their purchases. Toms created demand by blending consumerism with philanthropy, positioning their shoes as more than just a fashion statement but as a way to contribute to a larger cause.

As we navigate this complex web of social factors that drive demand, it's clear that consumer behavior is far from straightforward. The interaction between influencers, peer interactions, and cultural changes creates a rich environment where our wants evolve and adapt. Today's consumers are not just passive recipients of marketing; they're active players in a conversation about what's seen as desirable.

In this ever-changing landscape, brands need to be flexible, in tune with social trends, and responsive to the changing values of their audience. The challenges they face are significant, but so are the possibilities. By understanding the various social factors at play, businesses can create offerings that truly resonate with consumers, building loyalty and boosting demand.

Ultimately, the strength of consumer demand reflects our shared consciousness. It highlights not only what we want to buy but also what we care about as individuals and as a community. As we dig deeper into the subtleties of consumer behavior, it's clear that social influences—whether through influencers, peer dynamics, or cultural movements—remain central to shaping demand in a constantly evolving market.

Elasticity in Action: Product Demand Variability Explained

In the bustling marketplace, where the excitement of buying and selling interacts with the everyday choices of shoppers, the idea of elasticity plays a key role in how demand responds to price changes. Imagine strolling through a lively market packed with vendors selling everything from fresh bread to the latest gadgets, all trying to catch your eye and get you to spend your money. Now, picture a situation where the seller of your favorite organic coffee suddenly raises the price. Would you still treat yourself to that cup, or would you start looking for something cheaper? This simple question captures the heart of demand elasticity—how sensitive we are to price changes can greatly affect what we decide to buy.

At its essence, elasticity measures how much the quantity demanded of a product changes when its price changes. When we speak of elastic demand, we're looking at products where a small price increase leads to a big drop in how much people want to buy. On the flip side, inelastic demand describes products where price changes don't really affect how much people purchase. Knowing the ins and outs of elasticity isn't just important for economists and big business owners; it's also valuable for all of us as consumers. It helps us understand why some items fly off the shelves while others sit around collecting dust.

To bring this idea to life, let's think about two very different products: luxury handbags and basic groceries. Luxury handbags, often priced in the thousands, are usually considered elastic. When a brand like Louis Vuitton hikes the price of its famous handbag, it sends waves through the market. Some shoppers, drawn in by the allure of exclusivity, might still be willing to pay the higher price, but many others will start searching for cheaper options or decide to postpone their purchase. In this case, the demand is elastic because the price increase leads to a significant drop in how many people want to buy.

Now, let's compare that to something like bread. If bread's price were to rise by just a few cents, most shoppers would probably not think twice and continue buying it. After all, bread is a staple—a basic necessity for many, and it's not something easily swapped out, especially if it's a key part of their meals. The demand for bread is relatively inelastic because, despite a price hike, consumers will stick to their usual buying habits. Whether we're planning a family dinner or just want a slice to enjoy with soup, our need for bread stays strong, and our willingness to pay for it doesn't waver much.

Elasticity doesn't just affect individual purchasing choices; it extends its reach to entire markets, guiding pricing strategies and business decisions. Companies often analyze elasticity to set prices that optimize revenue without risking a loss of customers. For instance, if a soda company realizes its drinks have elastic demand, it might think twice before raising prices too high, knowing that even a small increase could lead to a noticeable drop in sales. Conversely, a pharmaceutical company making a life-saving medication might find that its product is inelastic; patients will pay whatever it costs because they need it, giving the company more room to adjust prices.

Real-life examples highlight how elasticity functions in our daily lives. When Netflix announced a price hike, many subscribers expressed their concerns. As consumers considered their options, it became clear that for some, the joy of binge-watching favorite shows outweighed the added cost. Yet, for others, the elastic nature of their subscription meant they were ready to explore alternatives like Hulu or even head back to traditional cable. Ultimately, Netflix had to carefully navigate elasticity, managing its pricing while keeping loyal viewers engaged.

The rise of discount retailers illustrates elasticity in action as well. Stores like Aldi and Lidl have found success by offering lower prices on everyday items, attracting shoppers who are sensitive to price changes, and might otherwise choose traditional grocery stores. Their ability to draw in price-conscious customers highlights the importance of demand elasticity—when shoppers see a better deal, they flock to the option that saves them money, reshaping the competition.

Branding also plays a crucial role in how elasticity works. Strong brands can create a sense of value that makes their products more inelastic. Just think about Apple and its iPhones. Many consumers are willing to pay a premium for the latest model because of the brand's reputation for quality and innovation. The emotional connection people feel and the status that comes with owning an Apple product can protect it from price-related demand shifts. Even if the price rises, loyal customers might stay committed, showing how brand loyalty can influence elasticity.

Let's not forget how cultural changes and trends can also impact elasticity. As social movements gain momentum, they can significantly change how consumers perceive products. For example, the rising demand for plant-based foods has affected the elasticity of meat products. As more individuals choose vegetarian or vegan diets, traditional meat items may see more elastic demand. A price increase for chicken or beef might push people to explore plant-based options instead. This shift not only highlights changing consumer preferences but also illustrates how societal changes can reshape market dynamics.

As we navigate the ever-changing world of consumer choices, it's clear that grasping the idea of elasticity is vital for individuals and businesses alike. For consumers, understanding how price changes influence purchasing decisions can lead to smarter choices, whether we're splurging on a luxury item or simply stocking up on groceries for the week. For businesses, understanding the nuances of demand elasticity can guide pricing strategies that balance revenue goals with customer loyalty.

Elasticity reflects our choices and motivations as shoppers. It highlights the delicate balance between what we desire and what we can afford, showing how price changes can shift our behavior. By recognizing the complexity of elasticity, we gain insights into the various factors that sway our buying habits, enabling us to navigate the marketplace with confidence.

As we wrap up our discussion on elasticity, let's remember that this concept isn't just an abstract economic idea; it's a living part of our everyday lives. Whether we're buying a new smartphone, picking out groceries, or planning a dream vacation, demand elasticity affects our experiences as consumers. By embracing this understanding, we empower ourselves to make choices that align with our values and budgets, leading to a more informed and engaged consumer culture.

Alfred Greene

Chapter 5: From Farm to Table: Supply Chains and Their Impact

Product Journey: Tracing Items from Origin to Sale

Understanding how products travel from their origins to our tables is more than just a logistical matter; it's a fascinating story that lies at the heart of our economy. Every item we encounter in our daily lives, whether it's a carton of eggs, a bottle of olive oil, or a pair of shoes, goes through an incredible journey. This process involves many people whose contributions often go unnoticed by the average shopper.

Let's start with a simple carrot. It begins its life deep in the earth, nurtured by sunlight, water, and the hard work of a farmer. We can call her Maria. Maria is the first link in the supply chain, and she pours her heart into her work. She carefully chooses the best seeds, practices sustainable farming, and watches over her crops with love. The taste and quality of her carrots depend on her dedication and respect for nature. Maria's connection to her land is much more than a job; it's a heartfelt bond with the soil that grows our food.

After the carrots are harvested, they need to be transported to a processing facility. This is where another group of dedicated people comes into play. Truck drivers, warehouse employees, and plant workers work together to ensure those carrots arrive safely and on time. It's like a well-rehearsed dance, where timing and communication make all the difference. If there's a delay, the carrots could spoil, disrupting the entire journey from farm to table. This is where we begin to see the complexities of the supply chain unfold.

Processing facilities, like the one where Maria's carrots go, are usually buzzing with activity. These centers are equipped with machines that clean, sort, and package the carrots for wholesale distribution. Every carrot that leaves this facility carries a story— a story of careful quality checks to guarantee that only the finest reach the supermarket shelves.

Take a moment to think about the importance of food safety at this stage. The carrots are meticulously inspected to ensure they are free from pesticides and contaminants. Processing plants must follow strict standards, building consumer trust when shoppers select that bunch of carrots. People are increasingly curious about where their food comes from, and they want to know the story behind it. If there's ever an issue, like a contamination scare, it's crucial for consumers and health officials to trace it back through the supply chain to find the source. A single error can create waves of consequences that affect not only the product but also the reputations of everyone involved.

Once the carrots are packaged, they're ready to be distributed. This is where wholesale distributors come in, acting like a well-oiled machine that connects producers with retailers. They have warehouses where products are stored until they can be sent to grocery stores or restaurants. These distributors build relationships with both farmers and retailers, managing deliveries and ensuring that supply meets demand. It's a tricky balancing act, especially when consumer preferences change suddenly or when unexpected events, like a storm, disrupt transportation routes.

When the carrots finally reach the grocery store, the spotlight shifts to the retailers. Creating an appealing display of fresh produce is an art form, designed to attract shoppers. The arrangement of the carrots on the shelves, the lighting, and the promotional signs all play a role in the shopping experience. Retailers, like Sam, a local grocer dedicated to his community, focus on sourcing products that are local and sustainably grown. Sam knows his customers appreciate that the carrots they buy come from nearby farms like Maria's. This connection builds loyalty; shoppers aren't just buying carrots; they're investing in a relationship that supports local agriculture and sustainable practices.

Transparency in the supply chain remains vital at this point, too. The stories of the farmers, the origins of the produce, and the cultivation methods are becoming essential parts of branding. Customers want to know who they are supporting with their purchases and increasingly prefer products that share a meaningful story. This shift in shopper behavior has encouraged retailers to highlight transparency in their marketing, showcasing their commitment to ethical sourcing.

In today's marketplace, technology plays a key role in providing visibility and accountability throughout the supply chain. Innovative tools, such as blockchain technology, are being used to track the journey of products from farm to consumer. Picture a shopper picking up a bunch of carrots and scanning a code that reveals its complete history—from the farm where it was grown, to the processing facility, to the distribution center, and finally to the store. Suddenly, those carrots are no longer just random produce; they transform into a testament to a well-managed supply chain, allowing consumers to make informed choices based on their values.

As we trace the journey of our carrots from the farm to the grocery store, we also need to recognize the broader significance of this path. Each stage of the supply chain relies on teamwork, efficiency, and a commitment to ethical practices. The connections among farmers, transporters, and retailers highlight how important every participant's role is in delivering the final product. For shoppers, understanding this journey is crucial for making choices that align with their values, whether that's supporting local farmers, prioritizing sustainability, or opting for products that have a smaller carbon footprint.

The concept of a supply chain might seem abstract at first, but when we look at the paths of everyday items, we uncover a rich story of human effort and various factors that influence what ends up on our plates. The carrots we choose are not just food; they symbolize the hard work, creativity, and dedication of everyone involved in their journey. As we become more aware of the intricacies of the supply chain, we arm ourselves with the knowledge to make better decisions—not just for our health, but for the well-being of our communities and our planet.

So, the next time you find yourself in the produce aisle, take a moment to appreciate the journey those bright carrots have made. Think about the farmer who nurtured them, the workers who processed and transported them, and the grocer who brought them to your local store. Each bite of that carrot tells a story—one that reflects the interconnectedness of our economy and the significance of transparency in our daily choices. Each carrot isn't just a product; it's a piece of a much larger puzzle in the intricate dance of supply and demand that shapes our world.

The Hidden Costs: Understanding Supply Chain Economics

Every time we look at a price tag, we're actually seeing the result of many decisions, actions, and often hidden costs that have built up over time. Supply chains aren't just a series of logistical steps; they are complex economic systems that affect us all. To really understand how these systems work, we need to look beyond just the prices we see and explore the layers of costs that build up at every stage of production. This knowledge can help us become smarter shoppers, making choices that align with our values and understanding of how the economy works.

Let's start by breaking down the different types of costs involved in the supply chain. At the very beginning are the raw materials, the building blocks of any product. Take the simple carrot, for example. The cost of growing these bright vegetables starts with the seeds, soil, and water that Maria, our hardworking farmer, uses to grow her crop. These raw materials come with their own price tag, which can change based on various factors like the season and weather conditions.

Next, we have labor costs. Maria's dedication is just one part of this expense. The labor involved in growing, harvesting, processing, and shipping the carrots adds another layer to the pricing puzzle. Every person who plays a role in this supply chain is essential, and they all need to be paid. Whether it's the seasonal workers who help pick the carrots, the team at the processing plant, or the truck drivers delivering the produce, every bit of labor is a necessary cost that needs to be considered.

Transportation costs are also crucial. Just think about how those carrots get from the field to the supermarket. This journey involves not only gas for the trucks but also maintenance costs, tolls, and driver wages. If a storm disrupts the roads or if fuel prices go up, transportation costs can shoot up quickly. These expenses are often a major factor in how much we pay for goods, especially for fresh items like fruits and vegetables that need to be delivered promptly to stay fresh.

Storage is another key element. After harvesting and processing, those carrots need to be kept in temperature-controlled environments to keep them fresh before they hit the shelves. The costs of warehousing include rent, utilities, and labor, all of which add to the final price we see at checkout. If there are delays in getting the carrots to the store, those costs can grow as the produce sits around, risking spoilage.

Marketing costs also play an important role in supply chain economics. The colorful packaging that catches our eye, the signs in stores promoting local produce, and the advertising campaigns designed to attract buyers all come with costs that eventually get passed on to us, the consumers. Retailers like Sam, who want to connect farmers with consumers, often invest in marketing strategies that boost the perceived value of their products. A carrot grown locally and sustainably can command a higher price, reflecting the costs of sharing that story effectively.

As we look at these various costs, we can distinguish between fixed and variable costs. Fixed costs remain the same regardless of how many goods are produced, like the rent for processing facilities. On the other hand, variable costs change based on production levels; for instance, the more carrots harvested, the greater the expenses for labor and transportation. Understanding the relationship between fixed and variable costs is crucial for grasping how pricing strategies are developed.

Take a bakery that makes carrot cakes. The rent for the bakery stays the same whether the bakers make ten cakes or a hundred. Yet, the ingredients—like flour, sugar, and those tasty carrots—are variable costs. As production increases, the cost for each cake may go down, demonstrating the idea of economies of scale. When a business can make more units without a significant rise in costs, it becomes more efficient and can offer lower prices to customers.

To see this concept clearly, imagine a graph showing the cost per unit against the number of units produced. As production increases, the cost per unit typically decreases, showing how larger production runs can benefit both the producer and the consumer. However, the opposite can also happen; if a bakery produces too few cakes, it may struggle to cover its fixed costs, leading to higher prices per unit.

The interplay of supply and demand adds another layer to this story. You can easily see seasonal price changes in grocery stores, especially with fruits and vegetables. When strawberries are in season, they may be affordable, but come winter, the price can skyrocket. This illustrates how supply and demand affect pricing. When there's plenty of a product, prices tend to fall. But when supply drops—due to bad weather, transportation problems, or seasonal factors—prices can rise sharply.

Take avocados as an example. A few years ago, avocados became a must-have in many diets, leading to a huge jump in demand. As demand soared, so did prices, creating challenges for consumers. The supply chain for avocados is complicated, with seasonal harvesting in Mexico and fluctuations in transportation costs, all of which impact what we pay at the store.

Real-life examples like these help us see economic principles in action. The complexities of pricing aren't just theoretical; they're part of our daily lives. We often find ourselves surprised by rising prices, but understanding the underlying costs can make sense of these changes. When we see that a rise in avocado prices might be linked to a poor harvest or higher transportation costs, we start to grasp the wider economic forces behind the scenes.

As consumers become more aware of these principles, they may begin to question why they pay what they do for different products. This awareness sparks critical thinking about buying choices. For instance, when faced with high prices for out-of-season produce, savvy shoppers might opt for in-season items, which supports local farmers and lowers their carbon footprint. Alternatively, they might choose frozen or canned goods, which often have lower transportation costs and a longer shelf life.

Moreover, the need for transparency in the supply chain is becoming increasingly important. More and more consumers want to know where their food comes from. This trend encourages suppliers to share stories about their products, from farm to table. When we understand the journey our food takes—from seeds planted in the ground to the hands that bring it to our grocery stores—we begin to appreciate the detailed network of costs and labor involved. This knowledge not only enriches our understanding of the products we purchase, but it also empowers us to make more informed choices.

Imagine walking into a grocery store and seeing a display of local produce with clear signs explaining each item's story. A bunch of carrots, for example, could have a card sharing Maria's story, the farmer who grew them, highlighting her sustainable practices and commitment to quality. This kind of transparency can influence our purchasing decisions, making us more willing to pay a little extra for products we see as ethical or environmentally friendly.

As technology continues to progress, we can expect to see even more improvements in tracking and transparency. Innovations like blockchain allow for precise tracking of products through the supply chain, making it easier for us to access information about what we buy. Picture a shopper scanning a QR code on a bag of carrots and discovering their complete history, from the day they were harvested to the journey they took to the store and the people who made it possible. Suddenly, shopping becomes a thoughtful exploration of how our economy is interconnected.

In this complex world of supply chain economics, it's vital for us as consumers to recognize the hidden costs tied to the products we buy. By understanding how raw materials, labor, transportation, storage, and marketing all come together, we can see how our choices impact not just our wallets, but the broader economy. Being aware of these principles encourages us to engage with what we consume in a more thoughtful way, prompting us to ask questions about sustainability, ethical sourcing, and community support.

The journey of goods from their origins to our homes reflects the intricate dynamics of supply and demand, shaped by many costs that add up along the way. By understanding these economic principles, we empower ourselves as consumers. We learn to value the products we choose, recognize the effects of our purchasing decisions, and contribute more consciously to the world we live in.

As we walk through grocery aisles and make choices about what to buy, let's keep in mind that every price tag tells a story. It represents the hard work, resources, and care that have gone into bringing those products to us. With this understanding, we can make informed decisions that align with our values, supporting not only our wallets but also the farmers, workers, and communities that are vital to the supply chain. So the next time you reach for that bunch of carrots or any other item, take a moment to appreciate the rich economics that have shaped its journey, and remember: every product has a story worth knowing.

Disruption Effects: The Impact of Weak Links in Supply Chains

When we think about supply chains, it's a bit like peeling an onion—each layer reveals complex interactions and connections that aren't always obvious right away. In recent years, we've seen just how fragile these networks can be. A series of unexpected disruptions have coursed through our economies, exposing weak spots that can shake the whole system. From natural disasters to political tensions, these vulnerabilities can have a major impact on businesses of all sizes, making it crucial to understand how disruptions flow through the economy.

Let's consider the damaging effects of natural disasters. Picture a hurricane roaring toward the Gulf Coast, bringing fierce winds and heavy rain. As the storm causes chaos, local businesses, such as shrimpers and oil refineries, find themselves struggling to stay afloat. In the aftermath, everything gets thrown into disarray: supply routes are blocked, facilities sustain damage, and workers can't make it to their jobs. What seems like a local crisis can actually have wide-ranging effects. For instance, restaurants in New York City that rely on Gulf seafood suddenly face shortages, leading to menu changes and higher prices for diners. This is a clear illustration of how interconnected supply chains can unravel due to a single disruptive event, sending shockwaves well beyond the initial incident.

The COVID-19 pandemic serves as an unprecedented example of how global supply chains can break down. As lockdowns began worldwide, factories shut down, shipping ports became overloaded, and people's shopping habits changed dramatically. This sudden shift led to shortages of essential items, from toilet paper to face masks. The pandemic highlighted the weaknesses in just-in-time inventory systems, which many companies had adopted to save money. Without much wiggle room, even small disruptions can snowball into big delays and shortages. Retail giants like Target and Walmart quickly adjusted by stocking up on essential items, changing their approach to build resilience in an uncertain market.

Geopolitical issues can also disrupt the delicate balance of supply chains. Take the trade war between the United States and China, for example. As tariffs were placed on various goods, companies that relied on Chinese manufacturers suddenly faced rising costs, forcing them to rethink their sourcing methods. For many, this meant searching for alternative suppliers, often in countries with lower labor costs but also less reliable infrastructure. This scramble impacted everything from electronics to clothing, making it clear that these interconnected systems are vulnerable not just to natural events but also to human decisions.

Real-world examples show how deeply these disruptions can affect both businesses and consumers. For instance, the semiconductor shortage that hit the automotive industry reveals the widespread consequences of vulnerabilities in supply chains. A fire at a Japanese chip factory in early 2021 set off a chain reaction across the global supply network. Car manufacturers, already dealing with the fallout from pandemic-related shutdowns, found it hard to get the crucial parts needed to build vehicles. Major automakers like Ford and General Motors had to cut back production, leading to significant financial losses and soaring vehicle prices. Consumers faced longer wait times for new cars, adding to their frustrations as demand for personal transportation grew.

The fragility of supply chains is evident in the food industry as well. When the Suez Canal was blocked by the Ever Given container ship in 2021, it created a ripple effect that disrupted trade routes worldwide. The grounding of the ship delayed countless deliveries, from electronics to everyday products, leading to shortages and price hikes in various markets. Grocery store shelves that once overflowed with options started to look bare, leaving shoppers confused about why their favorite items suddenly disappeared. This incident served as a stark reminder of how our modern economy relies on the smooth flow of goods. A single event far away can disrupt food availability, forcing consumers to face the reality that supply chains are fragile.

As businesses strive to bounce back from disruptions, there's been a growing focus on building resilience in supply chain planning. Companies are looking into ways to reduce risk by diversifying their supplier networks and adding backup systems. They're also reevaluating how technology and data analytics can strengthen their supply chains. For example, businesses can use real-time data to foresee potential disruptions and respond proactively, rather than waiting for problems to hit. This shift toward a more flexible approach helps companies adjust quickly to unforeseen challenges, ultimately improving their ability to weather storms— literal and metaphorical.

Additionally, the global push for sustainability is changing how companies manage their supply chains. As consumers become more environmentally aware, businesses must rethink their sourcing practices. The demand for ethically produced and eco-friendly products is prompting many companies to reassess their supply chains, emphasizing transparency and sustainability. This shift has significant implications for resilience. By building relationships with local suppliers or investing in greener practices, companies can create stronger supply chains that are less vulnerable to disruptions while also meeting consumer expectations.

Talking about resilience in supply chains is not just about dodging future crises; it's about realizing that disruptions are a natural part of a complex economy. The key lies in adopting a mindset that values flexibility and adaptability. Companies that build strong relationships with their suppliers and invest in technology are better equipped to handle shocks, while consumers who understand the interconnected nature of their choices can make smarter decisions.

In today's unpredictable environment, businesses are recognizing the need for a cultural shift. Resilience needs to become part of the company mindset, encouraging them to think about potential vulnerabilities as they plan ahead. Collaboration between departments, from procurement to marketing to finance, is crucial for finding and addressing weak links in the supply chain. By promoting open communication and sharing information, companies can develop a more unified strategy that boosts their overall resilience.

The fragility of supply chains is not just an abstract idea; it has real-time effects on businesses and consumers alike. Recognizing potential vulnerabilities helps us navigate the complex interaction between supply and demand. As we consider these disruptions, it's clear that our economy is always changing, influenced by many different factors. By acknowledging and tackling these weaknesses, we can forge a more resilient system that stands the test of time and turbulence.

Alfred Greene

Chapter 6: The Rollercoaster Ride: Why Prices Go Up and Down

Seasonal Influences: Price Variations Throughout the Year

Life moves in cycles, and each season brings its own unique colors, scents, and, interestingly enough, changes in prices. As the leaves transition from bright green to warm autumn shades, the costs of certain goods and services also start to shift, mirroring how people buy and what they want. To truly understand this, we need to look closely at the seasonal factors that cause prices to rise and fall, much like the thrilling ups and downs of a rollercoaster.

Imagine being a farmer during harvest time. Visualize a field bursting with ripe tomatoes, corn, and pumpkins just waiting to be picked. As summer fades and autumn rolls in, farmers get ready for the increase in demand. Families excited to whip up homemade salsa for backyard barbecues or to carve pumpkins for Halloween rush to local farmers' markets. The basic rules of supply and demand come into play, and prices for these seasonal favorites start to climb. A pumpkin that costs just a few dollars in September might skyrocket to double or triple that price by late October when everyone is looking for the perfect jack-o'-lantern.

Now, let's switch gears and think about the winter months. As the frost sets in, fields become empty, forcing grocery stores to depend on imports or produce grown in greenhouses. The price of fresh tomatoes in January can reach eye-popping levels, driven not just by transportation costs but also by the limited supply of these once-plentiful crops. Seasonal price changes aren't just about fruits and veggies; they ripple through different industries, influencing how we shop and what we pay for all sorts of goods and services throughout the year.

The idea of peak season versus off-season pricing really stands out in the travel world. Picture yourself planning a vacation to a sunny paradise. The thought of sun-drenched beaches and clear blue waters is hard to resist, but when you choose to go can significantly impact how much you'll spend on that flight. High season—often marked by school breaks and pleasant weather—sees prices soar as families and travelers hurriedly book their trips. For instance, a round-trip flight to Hawaii reserved in January for a June getaway could cost a family of four quite a bit. On the other hand, planning a trip during the rainy season or when school is in session can lead to great savings, allowing you to visit the same paradise for half the cost.

This push and pull between supply and demand during peak and off-seasons isn't just limited to travel; it's also evident in retail. The holiday shopping season serves as a perfect example of pricing tactics in action. Retailers, armed with colorful ads and tempting sales, gear up for the Black Friday rush. Prices on electronics, toys, and winter clothes drop before the holidays, all vying for the attention of eager buyers. Yet, once all the holiday decorations are put away, prices often bounce back to normal, sometimes even rising sharply as unsold stock has to make up for production and storage costs.

But let's not forget the more subtle seasonal pricing changes that can surprise shoppers. Think about seasonal treats that come with a higher price tag. Holiday-themed beers or festive pastries are often more expensive during the holiday season. A limited-time pumpkin spice latte at your favorite café might seem like a perfect seasonal treat in October, but its price reflects the seasonal excitement surrounding it. It's a mix of clever marketing and consumer habits, where limited availability and time-sensitive offers create an urge to buy.

Personal stories can offer great insights into how seasonal factors influence pricing.

Think about getting ready for a summer road trip. As you plan your route, you might notice gas prices swinging wildly as you drive through summer vacation hotspots. The lure of sunny beaches and mountain trails pulls in countless road trippers, sending demand—and prices—sky-high. You might fill up in a small town, only to find that when you cross state lines, the prices have shot up. Why does this happen? Seasonal demand and the number of travelers can create price differences that can leave you wishing you had planned your stops more wisely.

As we move through the seasons, let's also take note of the clever strategies businesses use to boost their sales. For example, retailers might kick off early bird sales to attract customers before the shopping frenzy peaks. This approach not only helps clear out stock but also takes advantage of the urgency shoppers feel, encouraging them to buy before prices go up. By adjusting their tactics to follow seasonal trends, businesses can create a win-win situation that keeps customers satisfied while ensuring they make a profit.

And what about the unpredictable weather? A sudden spring frost can throw agricultural prices into chaos, driving up the cost of strawberries and making you think twice before splurging on fresh fruit. Similarly, a drought can shrink supply, forcing shoppers to deal with higher prices at the grocery store. Climate-related events remind us that while seasons provide a useful framework for understanding price changes, unexpected factors can add complexity to the situation.

The relationship between these seasonal influences paints a colorful picture of the economy. As shoppers, grasping these trends not only helps us make better choices when we buy things but also shows us how supply and demand affect the economy as a whole. The next time you're at the grocery store or planning a trip, you'll have a better sense of how the seasons shape pricing, helping you make smart decisions that fit your budget and needs.

So, as we buckle up for the rest of this thrilling ride through the world of pricing, let's keep in mind that every twist and turn is shaped by the seasons that influence our lives. From summer barbecues to winter festivities, the prices we encounter reflect more than just supply and demand; they capture the lively dance of human behavior, nature's surprises, and the economic forces that touch our everyday experiences. Hold on tight; the adventure is just getting started!

Economic Cycles: Understanding Boom and Bust Trends

Life has its ups and downs, and the economy is no different. Just like our heartbeat, which rises and falls in a natural rhythm, economic activity goes through cycles—sometimes gradually, sometimes suddenly. By grasping these economic cycles, we can make better financial choices for ourselves and understand what drives the markets and affects prices. Think of the economy like a gentle wave, smoothly moving between highs and lows, reflecting the ongoing dance between growth and decline.

At the core of these economic rhythms are four key phases that every thriving economy goes through: expansion, peak, contraction, and trough. Each phase has its own unique traits and consequences, influencing how consumers behave, how businesses set prices, and even how governments formulate policies.

During the expansion phase, everything feels bright and optimistic. Consumers are confident, spending money freely, and businesses are excited to invest and grow. Jobs are plentiful, and GDP—our measure of economic health—shows strong growth. Companies launch new products, and the stock market usually does well, creating an overall sense of prosperity. Picture a busy shopping mall during this time: stores are overflowing, and shoppers are happy to pick up the latest gadgets, trendy clothes, and enjoy fancy meals. Prices often rise during these moments because demand outpaces supply, especially evident in the housing market where buyers are willing to pay top dollar for their dream homes.

But just like all good things, the expansion phase eventually hits a peak—the point where growth can't keep going. At this high point, we might start to notice signs like inflation creeping in, hinting that the economy is getting overheated. Businesses that were once thriving might become overconfident, producing more than they can sell because they think the good times will never end. As the market starts to change, consumers may become more cautious, affecting how they spend their money. The shopper who once eagerly purchased that shiny new SUV might now pause, considering whether it's really worth it.

As we move from peak to contraction, the mood shifts noticeably. The once-bustling mall may seem quieter, with more sales signs popping up as retailers try to get rid of excess stock. Unemployment rates begin to rise as businesses cut back on production or even close down. We see the effects of recession firsthand, hearing stories from friends and family who might be dealing with job losses or pay cuts. The economy feels less like a smooth wave and more like a wild rollercoaster, with sudden drops that leave many gasping.

The contraction phase can feel like a long, dark tunnel with little hope in sight. Businesses struggle to survive, and consumer confidence hits a low point. During this time, people change how they spend money dramatically. They start to postpone purchases, cut out luxuries, and prioritize saving. Even those who usually love to shop might think twice about buying that new gadget or dining out frequently. Instead, they might prefer cozy dinners at home or delay buying those tempting items.

Eventually, the economy reaches its trough, the lowest point of the cycle, characterized by high unemployment and stagnant growth. This phase can feel like the economy is on pause, but it also offers a chance for new beginnings. Slowly, the cycle will start to shift again. Sometimes government actions, like stimulus payments or tax cuts, are needed to help kickstart recovery. The key takeaway? Economic cycles aren't just abstract ideas; they have real effects on our everyday lives.

As we think about these phases, it's helpful to pay attention to the signs that indicate changes in economic trends. Unemployment rates are a good example; they can show us whether we're in an expansion or a contraction. When unemployment goes down, it often means the economy is growing, while rising unemployment suggests we're heading for tougher times. Similarly, when we look at gross domestic product (GDP) growth, we can get a clear picture of how the economy is doing. If it's consistently going up, that's a good sign, but a drop indicates trouble.

Inflation is another important factor to watch. A moderate level of inflation can mean the economy is healthy, but very high inflation or deflation can raise alarms. We can learn from past downturns, like the Great Recession of 2008, when soaring inflation met falling housing prices, leading to serious economic pain. Personal stories from that time highlight how families struggled to keep their homes and how some had to make tough decisions to get by.

Global events play a huge role in these economic cycles, adding another layer of complexity. For instance, think about the COVID-19 pandemic and its impact on markets worldwide. When lockdowns were implemented, economies came to a sudden halt. Businesses were forced to shut down, and consumer spending dropped dramatically, leading to a rapid contraction that caught many by surprise. In response, governments rushed to introduce stimulus packages to help soften the blow and jumpstart recovery.

Geopolitical issues can also create sudden changes. Things like trade conflicts, sanctions, and military tensions can disrupt supply chains and push prices up. The global economy is a delicate balance—just one ripple can affect distant countries. A great example of this is the 1973 oil crisis, which caused gas prices and inflation to rise sharply. Families had to navigate scarcity and rising costs, changing their daily choices in ways they never anticipated.

Given all these factors, understanding economic cycles is really important for consumers. Adjusting how and when we spend money based on the current phase can be financially smart. During expansion, for instance, it might be a good time to invest in stocks or make larger purchases, knowing that prices could rise. On the other hand, in a contraction phase, it's probably wiser to save money and hold off on non-essential buys, preparing for any financial bumps that may come.

Moreover, consumers can train themselves to spot the indicators of economic cycles. By keeping track of market trends, unemployment rates, and inflation, we can better handle the ups and downs of buying and spending in changing environments. As we observe the economy move through these cycles, it becomes clear that awareness and flexibility can be valuable tools.

Ultimately, the story of economic cycles is one of resilience and change. Each phase presents its own challenges but also offers chances for growth and renewal. By understanding these patterns, we can make smarter choices even when things are uncertain. So the next time you're thinking about a big purchase—whether it's that new car or a vacation trip—keep in mind the heartbeat of the economy and the beautiful, though chaotic, cycles it goes through. With understanding, you can navigate the twists and turns of the economy with confidence.

Commodity Fluctuations: The Drivers Behind Price Changes

The world of commodities is a fascinating and often confusing mix of change. One minute, the price of a barrel of oil might hit an all-time high, and the next, it could drop like a rock. These swings in commodity prices can seem random, much like a child's choices in a candy store, but if we take a closer look, we'll find a variety of factors at play that can greatly impact what we pay for everything— from gas to groceries. By understanding these factors, we can better grasp why prices go up and down, and how it all fits into our daily lives.

At the core of why commodity prices change is the classic economic idea of supply and demand. This straightforward yet powerful relationship shapes markets in ways that can surprise us. When there's too much supply and not enough demand, prices usually drop. On the flip side, when demand outpaces supply, prices tend to rise. But this basic relationship is influenced by many factors, all contributing to the ongoing push and pull of buying power and market behavior.

Take the oil market, for example. It shows perfectly how supply and demand work together. When tensions flare up in oil-rich areas, the fear of supply disruptions can send prices soaring overnight. Just a hint of a conflict—whether in the Middle East or due to sanctions against a major producer—can send shockwaves through global markets. Suddenly, consumers find themselves facing higher gas prices, which can increase costs for all sorts of goods and services that rely on transportation. The price at the pump isn't just a number; it reflects a series of effects that reach deep into our everyday expenses.

Natural disasters also play a big part in the ups and downs of commodity prices. When hurricanes hit, for instance, the oil and gas industry can feel the hurt right away due to damaged infrastructure and disrupted supply chains. A single storm can wipe out refineries, leading to less output and, consequently, higher prices. After such disasters, companies may raise prices to recover their losses, and these costs often get passed on to consumers. The global economy is so interconnected that even a local disaster can have wide-ranging effects.

Agricultural products provide another clear example of how outside factors can drastically change prices. Farmers depend on good weather to grow their crops, and when nature throws a wrench in the works—like droughts, floods, or unusual temperatures—the results can be severe. A bad harvest can create shortages, driving prices up. On the other hand, a bumper crop of corn or soybeans can flood the market, leading to lower prices. This volatility in agricultural commodities shows how consumer behavior can shift dramatically based on environmental factors we can't control.

Market speculation adds even more complexity to the pricing of commodities. Traders and investors often buy and sell commodities not just for their actual value but to make a profit off price changes. Speculation can create price bubbles, where the expected future value of a commodity pushes prices to silly heights. For example, during times of heightened demand for gold—often a safe choice in uncertain times—investors might inflate the price, regardless of actual supply. When that bubble bursts, the sudden drop can leave many people confused about what just happened.

These dynamics show that commodity prices are influenced by a wide range of factors that can change quickly. The back-and-forth of supply and demand becomes even more complicated with things like geopolitical issues, natural disasters, and market speculation. As consumers, it's valuable for us to pay attention to these changes, not just to protect our finances but to understand the broader impacts they can have.

The effect of commodity price changes goes beyond economics; it spills into our everyday lives. Rising oil prices, for example, can lead to higher costs for goods and services, because businesses pass on their increased transportation costs. This can contribute to inflation, squeezing household budgets and changing how we spend. We might find ourselves cutting back on nonessentials, choosing generic brands over name brands, or even skipping that long-awaited vacation to save a bit of money.

The realm of commodities isn't just a concern for economists and investors; it's something we all deal with as consumers. Understanding what drives price changes can help us make smarter choices. For instance, if we hear that oil prices are likely to rise due to geopolitical tensions, we might decide to fill up our gas tanks sooner rather than later. Or if a natural disaster threatens crop yields, stocking up on essentials before prices go up could be a wise move.

There are practical strategies we can use to handle these price swings. Keeping an eye on market trends, following news about commodity-producing regions, and being aware of seasonal cycles can help us anticipate price changes. Being flexible in our buying habits is crucial; if we can adjust how we spend based on current conditions, we can protect our finances better.

Additionally, it's important to realize that consumers aren't the only ones impacted by market fluctuations. Businesses have a role to play in managing their costs and setting prices. Companies that stay informed about upcoming commodity price changes can adjust their operations to reduce risk. Those that effectively manage their resources may be able to pass savings on to customers or at least keep price increases to a minimum when times are tough.

Ultimately, the world of commodity price changes reminds us that economics isn't just a bunch of theories and numbers; it has real effects on our daily lives. The prices we see at the grocery store, the gas station, and in the products we use are all tied to a complex web of factors that can shift quickly. By understanding these dynamics and educating ourselves, we can navigate the ups and downs of the commodity market with more confidence.

The main takeaway from looking at commodity price changes is that awareness and adaptability are incredibly important. As prices rise and fall, we need to change how we approach spending and saving. The more we know about what drives price changes, the better prepared we are to handle the financial ups and downs of everyday life.

In the end, grasping the ins and outs of commodity fluctuations is about more than just money; it's about seeing how our economy is interconnected and how outside factors can affect our personal finances. So, the next time you notice a price spike or a sudden change in the cost of something you regularly buy, take a moment to think about what's behind it. By doing so, you'll not only be a savvier consumer, but you'll also gain a better understanding of the complex dance of the economy we all participate in.

Chapter 7: Black Friday Bonanza: Special Events and Market Disruptions

Sale Psychology: The Economics of Major Shopping Events

Picture this: the day after Thanksgiving, and stores are buzzing with excited shoppers, each carrying bags filled with exciting finds. The atmosphere crackles with energy as people rush to snag the best deals of the year. Welcome to Black Friday, a true symbol of American shopping culture. This massive event, famous for its amazing discounts and huge crowds, is a gateway to understanding the clever psychology behind how retailers shape our buying habits and drive sales.

At the heart of this shopping frenzy is a fascinating interplay between supply and demand, where timing and emotions play crucial roles. Retailers have long tapped into human psychology, discovering powerful insights that enhance the shopping journey. For many, the thrill of scoring a highly sought-after item at a steep discount feels like a treasure hunt, sparking a sense of urgency. This urgency, often dubbed the "buying frenzy," isn't just a fluke; it's a well-crafted mix of marketing strategies designed to resonate with our basic instincts.

The idea of price elasticity comes into focus here, showing just how sensitive shoppers can be to price changes, especially during major sales. Discounts ignite hope and the desire for instant gratification. The lower the price, the more appealing the item seems, making it easier for people to make spur-of-the-moment buying choices. The excitement of a great deal, combined with the thrill of competing with other shoppers, turns everyday folks into enthusiastic participants in this shared shopping rush. The promise of saving money is often too tempting to resist, leading to a common feeling known as the "fear of missing out," or FOMO.

FOMO is like a pesky shadow lurking in the minds of buyers during events like Black Friday. It deeply impacts their purchasing choices, sparking anxiety that drives them to buy on a whim instead of making careful decisions. Retailers cleverly use countdown timers, alerts about limited stock, and one-day-only sales to crank up this sense of urgency. The idea that time is slipping away raises the stakes, creating a pressure that can push buyers toward hasty choices. Every second that ticks by heightens the fear that a great opportunity might slip away, leaving them regretting missed deals.

But the effects of these shopping habits go beyond just individual experiences. The collective actions of consumers influence market trends, shaping the economy as a whole. The sales figures from Black Friday can set the tone for retail in the months to come. A strong shopping season often boosts consumer confidence, signaling a healthy economy. On the flip side, disappointing sales during these crucial moments can create concern for retailers and investors, leading to a rethinking of pricing strategies and stock management.

As shoppers flock to stores and online platforms, they unwittingly become part of a larger experiment in market dynamics. Here, the dance between supply and demand takes the spotlight, with product availability directly linked to how engaged consumers feel. Limited-time offers create a sense of scarcity, fueling desires and motivations. The classic economic principle of supply and demand comes alive in real-time, as buyers react to what they perceive as value against a backdrop of limited inventory.

However, grasping the psychology behind sales is more than just about steering consumer choices; it's about recognizing changing expectations. As shoppers get used to the excitement of Black Friday, their future buying habits shift. The expectation that prices will drop during sales can lead to a behavior known as "waiting behavior," where shoppers hold off on purchases in hopes of snagging a better deal later. This waiting can have broad effects on overall market trends, causing temporary slowdowns in sales even for items that don't usually go on sale.

The impact of this psychological conditioning goes beyond individual shopping trips. It weaves into the very strategies businesses use, forcing them to adapt constantly to a marketplace shaped by consumer expectations. Retailers must innovate and find fresh ways to attract buyers, whether through loyalty programs, flash sales, or special promotions. The challenge is to create campaigns that not only spark quick sales but also build customer loyalty in a setting marked by ever-changing expectations and fierce competition.

As the holiday season draws near, the air fills with a mix of marketing buzzwords and promotional tactics, inviting consumers to engage. From creative campaigns to enticing offers, these approaches all share a common understanding of how people think and feel. The excitement of Black Friday, and similar shopping events, is built on a blend of anticipation, urgency, and the social nature of shopping. Shoppers often find themselves swept along by the enthusiasm of others, reminding us of the saying: "everyone's doing it." This communal vibe can amplify the urge to join in, blurring the lines between what we need and what we want.

What's more, the success of these strategies can be tracked in real-time through sales numbers and market data, offering insights into consumer behavior that were once hard to understand. Retailers keep a close eye on shopping trends, adjusting their tactics as needed to stay in sync with what their audience wants. Whether through targeted ads, personalized suggestions based on past purchases, or the thoughtful arrangement of products in stores, every element is carefully designed to spark a positive reaction.

As we make our way through major shopping events, it's crucial to remember that consumers aren't just passive recipients of marketing; they are active players in a complex economic dance. The psychological effects of shopping events resonate far beyond simple transactions, creating waves that influence everything from corporate strategies to big-picture economic indicators. Each purchase made on Black Friday is like a vote in the marketplace, reflecting personal choices and collective trends that shape retail's future.

In this intricate web of consumer actions and market dynamics, one thing is evident: the economics of major shopping events like Black Friday is a rich and layered story built from the threads of psychology, strategy, and human emotions. As retailers refine their tactics and shoppers respond to the lure of discounts, this landscape will keep changing, driven by the ongoing push and pull of supply and demand. Understanding these connections not only helps us navigate the chaos of shopping events but also sheds light on the broader impact of our buying choices within the grand landscape of the economy.

So, the next time you feel the buzz of excitement during a Black Friday sale, take a moment to consider the psychology behind your choices. Being aware of the forces at work not only empowers you as a shopper but also gives you a new perspective on the importance of each purchase you make. As you weave through the aisles, hunt for deals, and make decisions influenced by reason and emotion, you become a vital part of the ongoing story of supply and demand.

Disaster Economics: The Systemic Impact of Unexpected Events

The world we live in often feels like a tightrope walk, balancing the delicate scales of supply and demand. But all it takes is a storm swirling overhead, a sudden pandemic, or an economic slump to send everything tumbling into chaos. History has shown us time and again how unexpected events can shake economies to their core, disrupting markets and changing how people behave in ways that linger long after the immediate crisis has passed.

Let's take a moment to reflect on the Great Depression of the 1930s. This was a time when the stock market crashed in 1929, leading to an economic disaster that affected millions of lives. The shockwaves rippled through countless industries—from farming to manufacturing—resulting in massive job losses and widespread poverty. The economy, once thriving, felt like it was falling apart as supply chains broke and consumer confidence vanished. Businesses closed their doors, plunging a once-vibrant economy into despair. The Great Depression teaches us a critical lesson: the economy isn't just a series of numbers on a chart; it's a living, breathing system influenced by human actions and unexpected forces.

Now, let's jump to today. We're still dealing with the fallout from unforeseen events like the COVID-19 pandemic. At first, it seemed like a minor blip on the global radar, something few could imagine would escalate into a full-blown health crisis. The pandemic abruptly shut down economic activity. Lockdowns and social distancing turned our daily lives upside down, disrupting supply chains and changing how we shopped and interacted almost overnight. Grocery store shelves were wiped clean as people rushed to stock up, and businesses had to adapt quickly, often without warning. Our routines—how we shopped, dined, and connected—changed drastically, leaving many wondering if we'd ever return to the way things were before.

One vivid example of how disasters can ripple through an economy is Hurricane Katrina in 2005. This devastating storm hit the Gulf Coast hard, damaging oil refineries and infrastructure, and disrupting oil production significantly. In the wake of the hurricane, gas prices soared as supplies dwindled. Consumers faced rising costs, and businesses scrambled to adjust their supply chains. In a time when just-in-time inventory was the standard, this disruption starkly highlighted how fragile such a streamlined system can be when confronted with the unexpected.

The price hikes following Hurricane Katrina weren't just due to increased production costs. Market psychology played a huge role, too. When consumers sensed a scarcity, panic buying ensued, with people flooding gas stations even if their tanks were already half-full. The media often exacerbated this panic, fueling anxiety with reports about rising prices and dwindling supplies. The result? A market driven not just by supply and demand but also by consumers' fears and desires.

So, what happens after the initial chaos subsides? Once the panic fades, the effects of these disruptions often emerge in less obvious but just as important ways. Businesses adapt their strategies to cope with the new normal. Some succeed, quickly shifting their focus to meet changing demands. For example, during the pandemic, many companies that embraced e-commerce not only survived but thrived. Retailers who had relied solely on physical stores rushed to boost their online presence, leading to a surge in digital shopping. On the other hand, businesses that held on to outdated models faced serious consequences, with many forced to shut down for good.

This ability to adapt during tough times reveals a crucial fact about capitalism: it's not a stagnant system but rather a dynamic ecosystem that requires resilience and flexibility. The pandemic showed us just how fast consumer preferences can change, like the massive surge in demand for home delivery services and telehealth. Businesses that recognized these trends and pivoted accordingly not only survived but often came out stronger.

Consumer psychology plays a big part in these shifts. During crises, feelings of fear and uncertainty can lead to unexpected behaviors. Take the panic buying that swept through grocery stores at the start of the COVID-19 pandemic. Shelves were cleared as people rushed to stockpile essentials. This sudden demand led to shortages, further fueling consumer anxiety. On a psychological level, buying during uncertain times can give a sense of control, a way to cope with the chaos by ensuring we're prepared for whatever lies ahead.

The interaction between market disruptions, consumer behavior, and business adaptability creates a complex web that shapes the economy. The aftermath of crises can change market dynamics, establishing new norms that redefine what consumers expect. For example, the pandemic has made remote work and digital communication so common that it's unlikely we'll ever fully go back to the way things were. Companies are rethinking their office spaces and work setups, forever altering the employment landscape.

In times of unexpected turmoil, we often see a rise in what is known as "artificial scarcity." A clear example is the toilet paper shortage during the early days of the pandemic. As consumers rushed to stock up on essentials, retailers faced temporary shortages that created a perception of scarcity. This idea of limited supply spurred even more demand, leading retailers to impose purchase limits to curb hoarding. Ironically, this strategy designed to manage the crisis ended up reinforcing the very behavior it aimed to control.

The lessons learned from these crises are incredibly valuable for businesses trying to navigate future challenges. Agility and preparedness are crucial. Companies that foster a culture of innovation and adaptability are better prepared to deal with whatever storms come their way. It's not just about having a backup plan; it's about cultivating a mindset that welcomes change and sees challenges as opportunities for growth.

As we think about the widespread effects of unexpected events, we should also consider the broader implications for society. Economic disruptions can deepen existing divides, hitting vulnerable populations the hardest. After Hurricane Katrina, marginalized communities experienced a disproportionate share of the economic fallout, highlighting the challenges faced by those on the outskirts of the economy. Similarly, the COVID-19 pandemic has intensified inequalities, with low-wage workers and small businesses bearing the brunt of the impact.

In a world where change is the only certainty, understanding the relationship between unforeseen events and economic systems is crucial. The past offers valuable lessons for the future, allowing us to learn from the experiences of others. We must remember that the economy is more than just a collection of numbers; it's a reflection of human behavior shaped by emotions and life experiences.

As we navigate this unpredictable landscape, let's stay alert and flexible. The next crisis could be just around the corner. By learning from history and grasping how market dynamics, consumer behavior, and business strategies intertwine, we can better prepare ourselves for whatever challenges arise. Embracing resilience, fostering innovation, and adapting to change are not just survival tactics; they're essential for thriving in a constantly evolving economic environment.

Ultimately, the story of disaster economics is one of human resilience, creativity, and adaptability. It speaks to our ability to endure and to reinvent ourselves when faced with adversity. The insights gained from past events—both significant and minor—guide us as we navigate the unpredictable paths of modern economies. By acknowledging the importance of unexpected disruptions, we can better prepare for what lies ahead, advocating for systems that are resilient, equitable, and inclusive. The dance of supply and demand may be unpredictable, but with the right mindset, we can learn to lead rather than follow, turning challenges into chances for growth and renewal.

Artificial Scarcity: Corporate Strategies in Supply Limitation

Imagine if you could create a product that's only available in small amounts, making it even more attractive and valuable. This idea is at the heart of a marketing tactic used by various companies in different fields, known as artificial scarcity. It's not just a clever trick; it's a well-planned interaction between supply and demand, tapping into our human instincts to boost consumer interest. The basic idea is that when something seems rare, it instantly becomes more appealing. It's a bit like a mirage in the desert—always just out of reach, but so tempting that it makes you want to chase after it.

One of the most famous examples of artificial scarcity is the launch of limited-edition products. Take the fashion industry as a prime example. Brands like Supreme have really mastered this technique by releasing exclusive items that often sell out in minutes, leaving many customers racing to grab a piece of the desired collection. This creates a buzz, a whirlwind of excitement that sends demand soaring. The underlying message is clear: if you don't act quickly, you'll lose your chance. This sense of scarcity is carefully crafted, not just to boost immediate sales, but also to elevate the brand's status and build loyalty among customers.

Now, let's look at the tech world. Think about the launches of new iPhones by Apple. These events have become almost cultural milestones. When a new model hits the market, Apple often limits the initial stock, causing long lines outside their stores and major media coverage. They also use pre-orders to their advantage. By allowing customers to reserve their devices ahead of time, they create a sense of urgency—encouraging people to commit early, or risk being left out. The excitement around these launches isn't just about the new gadget; it's about the thrill of participating in something exclusive.

However, these strategies can come with a downside. While artificial scarcity can spark demand and boost sales, it can also lead to feelings of manipulation among customers. The boundary between clever marketing and exploiting consumers is quite thin. Take, for example, the Nike Air Yeezy sneakers designed by Kanye West. The initial releases caused such a stir that they led to accusations of price gouging and artificial inflation in the resale market. Many shoppers felt like they were in a high-stakes competition, with only the luckiest—or wealthiest—able to score a pair. Such backlash can damage a brand's reputation, transforming loyal buyers into frustrated critics.

In today's world, social media makes it easier than ever for customers to voice their concerns. Platforms like Twitter and Instagram can amplify dissatisfaction, and a brand's reputation can suffer in an instant. If shoppers feel they are mere pieces in a corporate game, their trust can vanish quickly. The infamous Fyre Festival serves as a warning. Marketed as a luxury music festival, it promised exclusivity and lavish experiences. But when reality fell short of the hype, the backlash was immediate and intense, leaving consumers feeling not just cheated, but outright manipulated.

The effects of artificial scarcity extend beyond just individual brands; they influence the larger market landscape as well. Economically speaking, when supply is limited and demand remains high, prices can skyrocket. This is especially evident in the housing market, where a shortage of homes drives prices up, making home ownership feel out of reach for many. This trend isn't just about real estate; look at the frenzy surrounding collectibles, like trading cards or limited-edition sneakers. The perceived value of these items often has little to do with how useful they are and more to do with the psychological impact of scarcity.

In economic terms, the laws of supply and demand suggest that when something becomes rare, its value should rise. But this can lead to an unstable market where prices don't truly reflect the actual worth of a product or service. Instead, they might mirror consumer perceptions and the intensity of marketing behind them. This is particularly noticeable with seasonal items, like holiday-themed merchandise. Retailers tend to stockpile these goods only to release them in limited batches. The outcome? A buying frenzy that can leave shoppers feeling either exhilarated or frustrated, depending on their luck.

Ethical questions arise around the practice of artificial scarcity. Should companies, motivated by profit, risk losing customer trust just to create an illusion of exclusiveness? This is a weighty concern for business leaders. A brand that aims to be exclusive must carefully balance maintaining desirability while ensuring consumers feel respected and valued. Being open and genuine becomes vital in achieving this balance. Brands like Patagonia have successfully built their reputation on sustainable practices and ethical sourcing, cultivating a loyal customer base that values both the products and the brand's mission. Their commitment to social responsibility allows them to engage in the scarcity game without facing backlash, as consumers recognize their sincere efforts to contribute positively to the world.

The idea of artificial scarcity also raises questions about long-term consumer behavior. Does the thrill of the hunt create lasting engagement, or does it lead to a cycle of disappointment? Often, consumers who repeatedly feel let down—whether due to missing out on desired items or seeing unfairness in the scarcity game—might choose to disengage completely. This disengagement can result in brand fatigue, where shoppers feel disillusioned and begin to explore alternatives that seem more genuine and accessible.

The broader implications of artificial scarcity can also be seen in the rise of counterfeit goods. As companies generate buzz around limited releases, some clever individuals produce fake versions of those coveted items. This underground market can harm not only the original brand but also consumers who unknowingly buy inferior products, deepening their feelings of mistrust.

As we peel back the layers of artificial scarcity, it becomes clear that this strategy has its pros and cons. While it can create excitement and boost sales, brands must remain aware of the ethical implications and consumer perceptions that can arise from such tactics. The companies that succeed will be those that can embrace the idea of scarcity while maintaining the trust and loyalty of their customers. The secret lies in finding the right balance—creating urgency without crossing the line into manipulation.

Imagine a marketplace where consumers genuinely feel valued instead of manipulated. This could change the dynamic between brands and their audiences, building lasting loyalty based on trust and transparency. The future of marketing might depend on companies realizing that nurturing relationships with consumers is just as important as generating demand for their products. Successful brands will likely focus on fostering community and connection rather than just pushing merchandise.

Ultimately, artificial scarcity reflects our societal values and behaviors. It shows how closely our purchasing decisions are linked to desire, status, and the emotional ups and downs that come with sales.

Understanding this complex interaction can empower consumers, helping them recognize when they're being played, allowing them to make informed choices.

Alfred Greene

Chapter 8: Digital Deals: How Technology is Changing the Game

E-commerce Evolution: The Shift from Physical to Online Shopping

The world of shopping has changed dramatically since the internet first came onto the scene. Remember the days when going to the mall meant spending hours searching for parking, navigating through crowded aisles, and waiting in long lines, only to discover the item you wanted was out of stock? Those days are fading fast. Thanks to e-commerce, our shopping habits have transformed, and the retail industry has been completely reshaped.

It all started in the early days of the internet with trailblazers like Amazon and eBay paving the way. Amazon launched in 1994 as an online bookstore, a small venture that quickly blossomed into a massive e-commerce platform, eventually offering everything from electronics to groceries. Meanwhile, eBay, which kicked off a year earlier, introduced us to the idea of online auctions, allowing people to sell their unwanted items to the highest bidder. These early successes showed that shoppers were eager to enjoy the convenience of purchasing items from the comfort of their own homes.

As e-commerce grew, secure online payment methods became a game changer. In the late 1990s, with worries about online fraud on the rise, services like PayPal stepped in to provide a safe way for people to make transactions online. Thanks to advances in encryption and security measures, consumers slowly began to trust online shopping, feeling confident that their financial information was secure. This trust was crucial for e-commerce to flourish, as it empowered shoppers to make purchases with just a few clicks.

With technology advancing, consumer expectations began to rise. Mobile shopping marked yet another turning point for e-commerce. With smartphones and tablets becoming commonplace, shopping transformed into an on-the-go activity. Mobile-optimized websites and apps made it easier than ever to browse products, compare prices, and make purchases anytime and anywhere. This convenience allowed for more impulse buying, as shoppers could quickly grab deals without much thought. Shopping shifted from a planned outing to a spontaneous decision, changing how we interact with retailers forever.

However, this change in consumer behavior hasn't come easy for traditional retailers. Many have faced challenges as foot traffic in physical stores decreased, struggling to adapt to this new digital world. The closure of once-iconic department stores and local shops is now a familiar story, as longstanding businesses find it hard to compete with the convenience and lower prices often found online. Some have chosen to create a hybrid model, blending in-person experiences with online options. Retailers started pouring resources into their e-commerce platforms, creating user-friendly websites and launching mobile apps to meet shoppers where they wanted to be.

Yet, for many traditional retailers, the shift to digital hasn't been smooth. The pressure to innovate is unrelenting, and simply having an online presence isn't enough anymore. Today's consumers expect personalized experiences, fast shipping, and easy returns. The competition is intense, with e-commerce giants like Amazon raising the bar high, challenging even the most established brands. So, how can traditional retailers not just survive but thrive in this increasingly digital landscape?

One approach many retailers are taking is to enhance the in-store experience, making shopping feel special rather than just a transaction. Some stores have transformed into experiential hubs, offering unique services, interactive displays, and expert consultations that you can't find online. By creating a welcoming atmosphere that encourages customers to engage with the brand, retailers can stand out and build loyalty.

Social media has also become a powerful ally for retailers trying to connect with consumers directly. Platforms like Instagram and Facebook have blurred the lines between socializing and shopping, enabling businesses to showcase their products through eye-catching images and targeted ads. Influencers have emerged as key players in this marketing landscape, using their following to promote products and drive sales. With more consumers flocking to these platforms, the potential for e-commerce keeps growing, and those retailers who tap into this power can connect with their audience in exciting and meaningful ways.

Looking ahead, it's clear that technology will continue to shape the future of e-commerce. From augmented reality apps that let shoppers virtually try on clothes to drone deliveries that can bring packages to your doorstep in no time, the possibilities are endless. The shopping landscape is always changing, and those who can anticipate and adapt will be well positioned for success.

The move from physical to online shopping is not just about technology; it reflects a deeper shift in how we think about value and convenience. With every click or tap, we're redefining the marketplace, challenging traditional ideas of supply and demand. Today, we have choices that go beyond geographical limits, and our preferences are shaping the rules of this digital game.

Retailers who recognize this change and embrace the opportunities it brings won't just survive the e-commerce surge—they'll thrive in it. Being adaptable, innovative, and focused on customers will unlock the full potential of this new shopping landscape. The evolution of e-commerce showcases the resilience of the industry and how businesses can reinvent themselves in times of change. We are on the brink of a new era, one that will continue to influence our shopping experiences and leave a lasting impact on the marketplace for years to come.

The Role of Algorithms: Unpacking Online Pricing Mechanisms

At the core of modern online shopping is a fascinating world of algorithms that quietly shape our shopping experiences. These complex lines of code act like the hidden architects of the digital marketplace, working tirelessly behind the scenes to perfect pricing strategies, sway buyer behavior, and ultimately increase sales. It's safe to say that algorithms are the unseen forces driving the e-commerce revolution, helping businesses thrive in a landscape that's both ever-changing and fiercely competitive.

Think back to your last online shopping trip. Maybe you compared prices on different websites and noticed that the same product had different prices depending on where you looked. Perhaps you experienced one of those "flash sales," where a price suddenly drops for a short time, creating an urgent need to buy. In these situations, algorithms are hard at work, constantly sifting through tons of data to find the best prices.

Dynamic pricing, a trend that has really taken off thanks to technology, is a perfect example of how algorithms are changing the game. You can picture it like a digital dance between supply and demand, where prices shift and change based on real-time information. Companies like Amazon have become experts at this dance, using their advanced algorithms to tweak prices multiple times a day—sometimes even several times an hour—based on changing demand, competitor prices, and shopping habits.

But how do these algorithms determine whether to raise or lower prices? The key is in the data. These systems draw from a wealth of information, including your browsing habits, past purchases, competitor prices, and current market trends. They analyze this data with complex mathematical models that help identify the sweet spot for maximizing both competitiveness and profits.

Imagine you're selling a product on Amazon, priced at $50. Suddenly, demand spikes after a popular influencer highlights your item on social media. An algorithm might choose to increase your price to $60 to take advantage of the extra interest. On the flip side, if a competitor lists a similar product for $45, the algorithm could quickly drop your price to keep shoppers interested. This balancing act is ongoing, resembling a high-stakes game of chess where every move is calculated with care.

But these algorithms do even more than just dynamic pricing. They also help create personalized pricing, which tailors the shopping experience to each individual. By analyzing data about customers—like previous purchases, browsing patterns, and demographic information—companies can develop personalized pricing strategies that resonate with each shopper.

Picture receiving an email from your favorite online store offering you a special discount on an item you've been wanting. That's the result of detailed algorithmic analysis that recognizes your loyalty and interest. By adjusting prices based on individual shopper profiles, retailers can enhance your experience while boosting their chances of closing the sale.

However, this raises important questions about data privacy and fairness. As consumers, we often trade our personal information for convenience, willingly giving up data for customized offers. But this practice brings up a crucial conversation about how far personalization should go. Is it fair for shoppers to pay different prices for the same product just because of their shopping habits? In many cases, it's a tough question to answer.

Let's think about how personalized pricing affects the overall consumer landscape. People who are less tech-savvy or lack a digital presence may miss out on great deals simply because the algorithms don't have enough data on them. Plus, as personalized pricing becomes more common, the risk of discrimination—whether intentional or not—grows. How can we create guidelines for ethical pricing practices that protect consumer rights while still allowing businesses to succeed?

This ethical issue becomes even more complicated by how quickly these algorithms work. The sheer scale at which e-commerce companies analyze data makes it nearly impossible for consumers to fully understand how their information is being used. As algorithms continue to advance and become more clever, the potential for misuse or misunderstanding of data becomes a real concern.

In response, many consumers are speaking out about their worries regarding data privacy. With the rise of privacy laws, like the General Data Protection Regulation (GDPR) in Europe and various state laws in the U.S., businesses are feeling the heat to be more open. But being transparent can have its downsides. While it builds trust, it could also put companies at a disadvantage by exposing their pricing strategies.

As we navigate this complex world, it's crucial for businesses to find a balance between using data for personalized experiences and respecting consumer privacy. Transparency, ethical practices, and consumer trust should guide companies as they refine their algorithms. The future of online pricing will largely depend on how well businesses can tackle these concerns while still pushing for innovation.

In the end, the role of algorithms in online pricing shows just how deeply technology affects our shopping experiences. As consumers, our choices are increasingly guided by unseen forces that dictate not just what we buy, but how much we pay for it. From dynamic pricing that responds to shifts in demand in real-time to personalized strategies that align with individual preferences, the impact of algorithm-driven pricing is both exciting and full of challenges.

As the landscape keeps changing, it's vital for consumers, businesses, and policymakers to engage in meaningful conversations about the ethical issues surrounding algorithmic pricing. By fostering a better understanding of how algorithms work and the data they depend on, we can empower consumers to make informed choices while encouraging businesses to adopt responsible practices that prioritize fairness and transparency.

The journey through the online marketplace is just getting started. As we explore the details of online pricing mechanisms, it becomes clear that our shopping experiences are not just transactions—they mirror our values and priorities in an increasingly data-driven world. The algorithms shaping these experiences may be invisible, but their influence is undeniable. As consumers, we must stay alert and navigate this new world of digital commerce with care.

The Sharing Economy: Innovative Supply Models in the Digital Age

Something fascinating is happening in how we buy and use goods and services: we're shifting from owning things to simply accessing them. The sharing economy has emerged as a powerful force, changing the way we shop by allowing us to connect directly with one another through digital platforms. In this new world, we don't just make purchases; we share, rent, and collaborate. This is a big change from older models where owning was everything and businesses controlled the resources to provide what we wanted. Now, technology lets us temporarily use what others own, creating a whole new way of thinking about consumption.

Take Airbnb, for example. It has completely transformed the hotel industry. Instead of staying in a bland hotel room that feels sterile and lifeless, travelers can now choose to stay in someone's charming apartment filled with unique decorations and a fully stocked kitchen. This personal touch is appealing to many, and it's all made possible by the digital platform that links hosts with guests. By letting individuals rent out their extra rooms, Airbnb has opened up a fresh category of lodging that is both affordable and accessible, while putting pressure on traditional hotels to rethink their offerings.

In a similar vein, Uber has shaken up the transportation industry. Gone are the days when you had to flag down a taxi or wait in line; now, with just a few taps on your smartphone, you can request a ride from a driver using their own car. This peer-to-peer approach has changed urban transportation for the better, giving riders more choices and providing drivers with flexible work opportunities. However, it also raises concerns about safety, regulations, and how traditional taxi services can survive in this new environment.

At the heart of the sharing economy is the idea of collaborative consumption—a concept that values access more than ownership. Thanks to technology, people can easily connect and interact in ways that weren't possible before. The rise of mobile apps and online platforms has made it simple for folks to borrow or rent resources from one another, leading to interactions that build community and trust. Whether it's getting a ride, renting a room, or swapping tools, these platforms turn everyday needs into collaborative experiences.

The way we think about pricing has changed too. Unlike traditional pricing models, prices on platforms like Airbnb and Uber are often flexible and can vary based on demand, location, and time of day. During busy travel seasons or big events, prices can soar, leading some to call it "price gouging." For example, if there's a major concert in town, be prepared for a spike in accommodation costs. While this pricing strategy reflects the dynamics of supply and demand, it can lead to discussions about fairness and accessibility.

To better understand these pricing changes, let's look at surge pricing, which Uber uses during busy periods. On nights when demand is high, like Friday at midnight, fares might double or even triple. At first, this might feel unfair, but it's a tactic designed to encourage more drivers to get on the road when they're needed most. Riders might grumble about the higher costs, but the alternative of long waiting times or no rides at all could make it worth it. This balancing act between demand and pricing is just one of many aspects that defines the sharing economy.

The sharing economy has not only influenced prices; it has also changed how we behave as consumers. With services like TaskRabbit or Thumbtack, people can hire freelancers for all kinds of tasks, from cleaning to graphic design. This trend towards outsourcing makes it easier to get help when you need it, often for less money than hiring someone full-time. Plus, these platforms let users rate and review service providers, creating a sense of transparency that builds trust.

However, this newfound ease also comes with challenges. How do you ensure the quality of services when they come from individuals instead of established companies? What happens if a freelancer doesn't meet your expectations? In traditional models, companies take on most of the responsibility, but in the sharing economy, consumers often have to do their homework to find reliable providers. This raises important questions about consumer protection and the need for rules that adapt to these new ways of doing business.

As we think about what's next for the sharing economy, we see that traditional businesses are facing significant challenges. Established industries need to rethink their strategies if they want to stay relevant in a world where people increasingly prefer access over owning something. Companies that stick to outdated models may find themselves falling behind as more consumers choose shared solutions that offer cost savings and the excitement of community engagement.

For instance, many hotels are beginning to evolve by offering unique experiences, like boutique hotels that highlight local culture and provide personalized service.

Car rental companies are also looking into peer-to-peer car-sharing services to meet the growing demand for flexibility and convenience. These adaptations show that while the sharing economy poses challenges, it also opens doors for creativity and growth.

We can expect that regulations will change in response to these shifts. Policymakers will need to tackle the challenging task of developing rules that cover safety, workers' rights, and consumer protection in a world where business models are changing quickly. For example, as ride-sharing becomes more common, local authorities might need to set licensing and insurance standards to keep passengers safe. Finding a balance between encouraging innovation and protecting consumers will be key to a sustainable future.

Looking to the future, there seems to be no limit to how much the sharing economy can grow. As technology continues to move forward, new platforms and services will pop up, changing how we interact with the things we need. From shared office spaces like WeWork to platforms that let us rent high-end fashion, the sharing economy is set to redefine how we think about consumption in many ways.

However, we must also be mindful of the consequences of this growth. While sharing can help reduce waste and promote sustainability, it also raises concerns about how we manage the shared resources we're increasingly relying on.

The sharing economy paints an exciting picture of a future where technology builds community, enhances access, and promotes innovative supply models. As consumers, we get the chance to engage in a marketplace that prioritizes collaboration and connection, making our shopping experiences more meaningful. By embracing these changes, we can reshape what it means to consume in the digital age, creating an environment that values sustainability, accessibility, and shared responsibility.

Chapter 9: Government in the Mix: Regulations and Their Effects

Price Controls: Government Intervention in Markets

Government involvement in markets can feel like a double-edged sword. It tries to navigate the tricky waters of supply and demand but also risks upsetting the balance it aims to create. Price controls are one of the most common tools in this regulatory toolbox, created to tackle extreme situations that can lead to unfair pricing. By putting in place price ceilings and price floors, governments hope to shield consumers from wild price swings and ensure that producers receive fair compensation. However, while these interventions come from a good place, they can sometimes lead to unexpected problems, changing the economic landscape in ways that don't match the original goals.

Let's look at rent control as an example. In crowded cities like New York or San Francisco, where the demand for housing often surpasses what's available, local governments have put rent control measures in place to protect tenants from high rental prices. The goal is admirable: to offer stability to families and individuals who might otherwise be pushed out of their homes. However, the reality of rent control is more complicated. While it keeps prices lower for those lucky enough to find a rent-controlled apartment, it also makes landlords less inclined to maintain their properties or invest in new buildings. Over time, this can lead to a decline in housing quality and a drop in new housing options, making the very issue it was meant to solve even worse.

The effects of price ceilings don't just stop at rental markets. Think about minimum wage laws, which are a type of price floor aimed at protecting workers from low pay. At first glance, a higher minimum wage seems great—who wouldn't want to earn more? But in reality, setting the minimum wage too high can lead to job losses, as businesses struggle to afford their employees. This might create a situation where there are more people looking for work than there are jobs available. Ironically, the very workers the law aims to help might find themselves in a tougher situation, facing unemployment or underemployment.

When governments put price controls in place, they often dream of a fairer distribution of resources. But the economic effects can be trickier than expected. During crises—like natural disasters or health emergencies—governments might set price ceilings on essential items like food and medical supplies to stop price gouging. While this could offer quick relief to consumers facing rising prices, it can also lead to shortages. Suppliers might be unwilling or unable to sell their products at these low prices. When a price is kept below what the market would usually set, demand can spike, but supply often can't keep up, resulting in bare shelves and unhappy customers.

The insights we can gather from price controls are crucial for navigating the economy. These measures can provide temporary help or protect those in need, but they can also cause problems that complicate market behavior. Understanding the delicate balance of supply and demand is important; price controls don't work in isolation. The broader effects of these policies can ripple throughout the economy, impacting both consumers and producers.

Real-life examples highlight the unexpected fallout from price controls. Take Venezuela, for example, where the government imposed strict price controls on essential goods to tackle inflation and protect consumers. At first, this seemed like a smart move; however, it quickly led to severe shortages as producers struggled to make a profit under the mandated price limits. The outcome was a devastating economic collapse, with people facing empty shelves and a booming black market where goods were sold at much higher prices than the controlled rates. This situation illustrates how well-intentioned attempts to stabilize prices can quickly turn into chaos when market signals are ignored.

As we think about the complexities of price controls, it's important to understand the economic reasoning behind these actions. Economists talk about market equilibrium, which is the point where supply and demand meet. When price ceilings and floors are introduced, they disturb this balance, causing imbalances that can echo throughout the economy. The challenge is to know when and how to step in without causing more harm than good.

The political scene often adds another layer of complexity to the conversation about price controls. Policymakers might chase short-term wins instead of focusing on long-term economic health, leading to rushed decisions that overlook solid economic analysis. In the rush to respond to public concerns about rising prices or low wages, the finer points of economic theory can be overlooked, resulting in policies that could be harmful in the future. It's vital to take a thoughtful, informed approach to regulation, especially as we see how government choices impact daily lives.

Moreover, the effects of price controls can reach far beyond the specific market they aim to influence; they can have wide-ranging impacts across entire economies and even internationally. The agricultural sector, for instance, often feels the weight of government actions. When price controls are put on staple crops like corn or wheat, it can disrupt not just local markets, but international trade as well. Countries that depend on agricultural exports may find their farmers struggling to stay afloat, leading to a drop in both quality and quantity of produce available for local needs and global markets. This disruption can create ripple effects that impact food security in places far removed from where the price controls were applied.

In the end, the story of price controls is a complicated one, filled with both success and struggle. It serves as a powerful reminder of the fragile balance within economies and the significant role government intervention plays in maintaining that balance. As we sift through the intricacies of supply and demand, it becomes clear that understanding price controls is crucial for anyone looking to grasp how markets really work. The interaction between government regulation and market forces is a delicate dance, one that shapes the economic futures of individuals, businesses, and entire nations.

As we think about the mixed outcomes of price controls, it's also important to realize that their success depends on the larger economic context. In a strong economy, price controls might cause only minor disruptions, while in a weaker one, they can worsen existing inequalities and contribute to economic struggles. The key is to find the right balance between protecting consumers and letting markets function freely.

Ultimately, exploring price controls teaches us a vital lesson about government intervention: it's rarely just a matter of right or wrong. It requires a nuanced grasp of economic principles, an awareness of potential outcomes, and a willingness to adjust policies in response to changing economic situations. The delicate interplay of supply and demand, government regulation, and market forces creates a complex web that shapes our economic reality. Navigating this landscape calls for an openness to engage with these complexities, recognizing that the journey toward fair pricing is often filled with challenges and surprises.

Taxation and Subsidies: Distorting Supply-Demand Dynamics

Government involvement in markets can take many forms, but two of the most powerful are taxation and subsidies. These tools can shape how the economy works in profound ways, influencing the balance between supply and demand. While taxes are often seen as necessary for funding public services, they can also raise production costs for businesses, which can lead to higher prices for consumers and changes in how the market operates. On the other hand, subsidies are designed to encourage production and consumption by cutting costs, but they can create distortions in the market that make things less efficient.

When a government decides to tax a specific product or service, the effects are often quick and noticeable. The price for that good typically goes up, causing a shift in what consumers want. For example, if a tax is placed on sugary drinks to tackle obesity, it might reduce the number of people buying those beverages. However, this could also hurt the companies that produce them, leading to lower sales and potentially costing jobs in an industry already under pressure.

This unintended outcome highlights the tricky relationship between government policies and the market. Although the reasoning behind such taxes might be good, the results can tell a different story. When prices rise, consumers often change their buying habits. They might buy less, switch to cheaper options, or even stop buying certain items altogether. For producers, this creates a tough situation: they not only see fewer sales but also have to adapt their businesses to meet the changing preferences of consumers.

Taxes can also shift market equilibrium, which is a key idea in economics that refers to the balance point where supply and demand meet. When a tax is imposed and prices go up, the market might find itself in a new, unstable state. As consumers pull back, producers might cut back on how much they supply. This can create a mismatch between what buyers want and what's available, leading to instability that can create bigger economic issues, especially in industries already facing challenges.

On the other hand, we have subsidies—government support aimed at helping certain businesses or sectors. Subsidies can lower production costs, encouraging companies to produce more and potentially lowering prices for consumers. A good example of this is the agricultural sector, where farmers often get financial help to grow staple crops like corn or soybeans. This support can lead to increased production in the short run, making prices at the grocery store more affordable. Sounds good, right? But the reality can be quite different.

When production is artificially boosted by subsidies, it can create market imbalances. Farmers, pushed to grow as much as possible, might overlook the benefits of diversifying their crops or adopting practices that could be better for both the environment and the economy. This can lead to a situation where there's too much of one product, resulting in waste and inefficiencies. Over time, this can hurt both farmers, who find themselves in a crowded market, and consumers, who may end up with fewer choices in what they buy.

Looking at real-world examples can show us just how dramatic the effects of taxation and subsidies can be. Take the American sugar industry, for instance. Sugar producers in the U.S. have long enjoyed significant subsidies and protections from foreign competition. These policies were intended to help local farmers and stabilize the sugar market. However, they have led to sugar prices in the U.S. being much higher than those in other countries, which burdens consumers and creates a system that discourages innovation and efficiency in the industry.

Moreover, the effects of subsidies aren't limited to just immediate economic benefits. They can also encourage practices that harm the environment. For example, in farming, the reliance on growing a single crop, known as monoculture, can be worsened by subsidies. This approach can harm the soil, make crops more vulnerable to pests, and reduce biodiversity. What starts as a good intention to stabilize prices can end up causing long-term damage to the ecosystems that our agricultural systems rely on.

As we think about how taxation and subsidies interact in the marketplace, it's clear we need to be thoughtful about government interventions. Policymakers have to balance the intended benefits with the potential negative consequences. A tax on sugary drinks may promote healthier choices, but it could also hurt producers and lead to job losses in that industry. Similarly, while agricultural subsidies might make food cheaper in the short term, they can disrupt market signals and create a reliance on government support.

Understanding how taxation and subsidies work together means looking at the bigger picture. It's not just about what happens immediately but also about the long-term effects on the economy and supply-demand relationships. Finding the right balance between helping consumers and supporting producers is tricky. Short-term fixes can lead to long-term problems.

Exploring different case studies on taxation and subsidies reveals a range of outcomes that reflect the complexities of government involvement in the market. For instance, in the renewable energy sector, subsidies have been put in place to promote switching from fossil fuels to renewable energy sources. While initially celebrated for encouraging innovation and cutting carbon emissions, these subsidies can also distort the market. Some companies that rely heavily on government funding may struggle to compete in an open market, leading to inefficiencies and a lack of real innovation.

In another case, housing subsidies are meant to make homeownership more attainable. Although they can help people buy homes and boost the housing market, they can also drive up property prices as more buyers enter the market. When many buyers have financial help, it can create a bidding war that increases prices, which can counteract the benefits of the subsidies for many potential homeowners. This situation shows how subsidies can sometimes contribute to the very problems they aim to solve.

The challenges of taxation and subsidies highlight how significant government involvement is in shaping market dynamics. While these tools can lead to positive changes, they can also bring about unintended consequences that ripple through the economy. As policymakers work through the intricate relationships of supply and demand, they need to keep an eye on the broader implications to create effective and lasting solutions.

Ultimately, the story of taxation and subsidies goes beyond just the mechanics of government actions; it's about the real people whose lives are impacted by these decisions. The effects reach deep into everyday life, influencing everything from what we buy to how many jobs are available and even how sustainable our environment is. Finding the right balance between supporting industries and nurturing a fair, competitive marketplace remains a tough challenge. As we look at these economic forces in action, it becomes clear that the road to effective government intervention is filled with complexities and requires constant attention and flexibility.

Trade Policies: The Global Impact on Local Pricing

In our interconnected global economy, trade policies act like the threads that link countries, businesses, and consumers in a constantly changing marketplace. Although it may seem like the world is getting smaller thanks to advancements in technology and transportation, the reality of international trade is often complicated and filled with challenges. Governments around the world use various tools to shape market dynamics, protect local industries, and affect local pricing. Among these tools, tariffs and quotas stand out, each bringing its own set of effects and unexpected consequences.

Tariffs have become a familiar term in the world of international trade. These are essentially taxes placed on imported goods, and their main purpose is to make foreign products more expensive than those made at home. This encourages shoppers to choose local items instead. Imagine standing in a grocery store, deciding between two cans of tomatoes: one costs $1.50 and the other $2.00. If the cheaper can is from Italy and a $0.50 tariff is added to it, the price rises to $2.00, making it equal to the domestic option. The goal is that shoppers will go for the local can, thus supporting our farmers and manufacturers.

However, the effects of tariffs go far beyond the grocery store. A current example is the tariffs on steel and aluminum imports in the United States. These tariffs were meant to support local manufacturers and protect jobs in the steel industry, but they have created a ripple effect across many sectors that rely on these materials. Industries like construction and automobile manufacturing, which need steel and aluminum, have seen their production costs soar. As these costs increase, consumers end up paying more for everything from cars to kitchen appliances and even infrastructure projects.

Take the example of building a new home. Builders usually buy steel for the framework and aluminum for the windows. When tariffs are imposed, the increased prices for these materials can lead to a significant rise in the overall cost of a new home. Homebuyers, already facing rising mortgage rates and growing demand for housing, find their options becoming less affordable. This situation shows how even a seemingly simple decision to impose tariffs can lead to a complicated chain of events that affects many parts of the economy.

Additionally, tariffs can trigger retaliation from other countries, leading to trade wars that create further tension and disrupt pricing structures. When one country raises tariffs, affected partners often respond with their own tariffs on goods imported from that country. This back-and-forth can escalate into a tense trade environment, hurting consumers everywhere. The end result? Higher prices and fewer choices as markets split apart and competition diminishes.

Quotas are another type of government action that greatly influences local pricing. Unlike tariffs, which raise the price of imported goods, quotas limit how much of a product can be imported into a country. By setting a cap on the supply of foreign products, quotas can create scarcity and push prices higher. For instance, think of a popular brand of coffee with a limited import quota. Once the quota is filled, consumers wanting that specific coffee will either have to pay a premium price or opt for a less-known alternative. As demand stays steady but supply is restricted, shoppers find themselves caught between what they want and what's available.

The impact of quotas is especially clear in industries where demand is high and competition is tough. Take the dairy industry, for instance. Some countries set quotas to protect local dairy farmers from international competition. While this might be intended to help domestic producers, it can also lead to higher prices for consumers. Under quotas, shoppers often have fewer choices in dairy products, as only a limited quantity can enter the market. This situation can mean consumers either pay higher prices for local products or miss out on foreign options altogether.

Quotas can also lead to tensions in international relations. A country that imposes strict import quotas may face backlash from its trading partners, who might see these measures as unfair protectionism. This can lead to diplomatic strife and retaliation, creating a cycle of conflict that undermines cooperation. The looming threat of trade wars puts both consumers and businesses in a difficult position.

As we explore the details of tariffs and quotas, it becomes clear that understanding trade policies is vital for both consumers and businesses. Being informed about how these policies work helps us navigate the complexities of the global economy. For consumers, knowing how tariffs and quotas affect prices can influence buying choices. When faced with higher costs, consumers might choose to back local products, but they should also think about the wider impact of their decisions on the market.

For businesses, the stakes are even greater. Companies need to keep an eye on changes in trade policies that can directly influence their production costs and competitiveness. A sudden hike in tariffs might mean rethinking supply chains, finding new materials, or adjusting pricing strategies to stay in the game. Successfully navigating the challenges of international trade takes flexibility and foresight, as businesses adapt to the constantly shifting landscape of government policies and global market trends.

The connection between trade policies and local pricing highlights the importance of engaging thoughtfully with these issues.

Policymakers must find a careful balance between supporting domestic industries and ensuring fair prices for consumers. While tariffs and quotas can protect jobs and promote local production, they can also create unexpected consequences that ripple through the economy.

As we navigate the complexities of today's economy, we should recognize that trade policies are more than just abstract ideas confined to government discussions. They have real impacts on the lives of millions, shaping the prices we pay for essential goods and services. Understanding how government actions interact with market dynamics enables us to make informed choices as consumers and advocates for fair trade practices.

In an age of growing globalization, decisions made at the national level carry weight beyond borders. Trade policies can influence entire industries, sway consumer behavior, and even affect international relations. By staying informed and attentive, we can better navigate the intricate web of the global marketplace and push for policies that create a fairer and more just economic environment.

Alfred Greene

Chapter 10: Crystal Ball Economics: Predicting Future Trends

Economic Indicators: Understanding Signals of Changes

When it comes to understanding the ups and downs of our economy, economic indicators act like lighthouses, guiding us through the fog of uncertainty. These numerical signs light the way, offering insights into the health of our markets and helping us make important financial decisions. There are three main types of indicators: leading, lagging, and coincident, each playing a unique role in how we grasp economic trends. Think of them as a trio of advisors, each providing a different viewpoint on what's happening now and what could be just around the corner.

Leading indicators are like a forward-looking compass, giving us a sneak peek at potential future economic activity. They signal changes that might come before most people notice them. For example, the stock market is often viewed as a measure of investor confidence; it tends to react to expectations about future profits. When investors feel good about a company's earnings, stock prices usually go up, suggesting a positive economic outlook. While this connection isn't always perfect, it offers valuable insights into the direction the economy might take.

Aside from the stock market, other leading indicators can paint a clearer picture of future trends. New housing starts are one such sign; when builders begin constructing new homes, it often shows that consumers are feeling more confident and ready to spend. Similarly, manufacturing orders act as a hint of upcoming economic activity. If companies are ordering more materials, it indicates they expect demand to rise and plan to increase production. Consumer sentiment surveys also play a crucial role—when people feel optimistic about their financial futures, they're more likely to spend, which helps the economy grow.

Learning to understand leading indicators helps us better read the economic landscape and anticipate important changes. Imagine being able to spot the next big trend in technology or consumer behavior before it becomes mainstream—this skill could lead to smart business decisions or wise investments.

On the other hand, lagging indicators tell a different story. They act like historians of economic data, confirming trends that have already happened. Unemployment rates, for instance, show the state of the job market but do so with a delay. When unemployment starts to rise, it often means the economy is already in a downturn, as businesses cut back on hiring or lay off workers in response to decreased demand. Corporate profits also fall into this category; they show whether companies were successful in past quarters or years, but they don't give clues about future performance.

These indicators are vital for evaluating how effective past economic policies and decisions have been. Policymakers and economists closely examine lagging indicators to measure the impact of their actions. If a government introduces measures to boost job creation and the unemployment rate falls afterward, those lagging indicators confirm that the strategies worked. However, it's important to remember that, since they confirm trends after the fact, lagging indicators may only provide limited help in making future decisions.

The third type, coincident indicators, gives us a snapshot of the current economy. This is where metrics like GDP growth and personal income levels come into play. Coincident indicators work in real-time, allowing us to understand the economy's strength at any moment. When GDP is rising, it suggests a growing economy; conversely, if real GDP shrinks, it usually indicates a recession. Personal income levels also reflect economic health since higher incomes typically lead to more consumer spending, which drives economic growth.

Grasping coincident indicators allows individuals and businesses to evaluate their immediate economic surroundings. For example, a small business owner keeping an eye on personal income levels can decide whether to increase production in anticipation of rising consumer demand. Similarly, investors analyzing GDP growth can make educated choices about whether to invest in riskier assets or take a more cautious approach.

To illustrate how these indicators play out in real life, think about a tech company getting ready to launch a new product. By looking at leading indicators, the company can assess consumer sentiment surveys to see if the market is ready for their innovation. If sentiment is positive and manufacturing orders in their sector are rising, they might choose to ramp up production. But if they notice rising unemployment rates among their target customers, they could rethink their launch plan or adjust their marketing strategy.

There are plenty of examples showing how smart investors and businesses have used these indicators to their advantage. For instance, if an investor closely tracks new housing starts and sees an increase in construction in a specific area, they might decide to invest in real estate or related sectors, expecting that new residents will boost the demand for housing and services.

Larger companies may also use lagging indicators to evaluate how well their past strategies worked. After a company implements cost-cutting measures, it could look at its corporate profits in the following quarter. If profits rise, that could indicate their approach is effective, leading them to either continue those measures or reinvest the savings back into the business.

In the world of economic forecasting, combining insights from leading, lagging, and coincident indicators enables people to make better-informed decisions. While no indicator is perfect, understanding their differences gives us a fuller picture of the economic environment. Just like a skilled sailor reads the winds and tides to navigate the seas, an insightful investor or business leader can interpret these signals to chart a successful course.

In a world where economic conditions can change quickly, paying attention to the signals from these indicators is invaluable. The relationship between leading, lagging, and coincident indicators creates a framework for understanding not just where we are, but also where we might be headed. Economic indicators are more than mere numbers; they reflect our collective behaviors, decisions, and the intricate balance of supply and demand that shapes our marketplace.

With the right knowledge and tools, navigating the complexities of the economy becomes much more manageable. By developing skills in reading these indicators, individuals can make well-informed financial choices that benefit not just their own interests but also help deepen their understanding of the economic world around them. The key to prediction lies in our ability to observe, interpret, and act on the signals the economy sends our way.

Spotting Opportunities: Emerging Markets and Future Prospects

In the constantly changing landscape of our global economy, being able to spot emerging markets and investment opportunities feels like having a special radar that picks up on trends before they catch on. These opportunities aren't just sitting around, waiting for us to find them; they're often right in front of us, waiting for someone with the insight to see them. With the right tools, we can navigate this ever-evolving terrain and make the most of the shifts in supply and demand that will shape our economic future.

The first step to recognizing these opportunities is grasping how to identify emerging markets. What does it mean to be "emerging"? Simply put, it refers to sectors or industries that are on the verge of growth, often spurred by advances in technology, changes in demographics, and shifting consumer preferences. Picture it like a garden: some plants are well-established and thriving, while others are just beginning to break through the soil, poised to bloom with a little nurturing.

Take the renewable energy sector, for example, which has seen explosive growth in recent years. This isn't just a passing trend; it's a major shift driven by society's growing focus on sustainability. In the past, fossil fuels ruled the energy market, but as more people become aware of climate change and environmental issues, renewable energy sources—like solar, wind, and hydroelectric power—are stepping into the spotlight. Investors and entrepreneurs who notice these changes early can reap huge rewards. For instance, companies that specialize in solar panel production or innovative battery storage solutions have moved from being niche players to essential players in the energy field, drawing in significant investment and consumer interest.

But finding emerging markets involves more than just keeping an eye on energy trends. It requires a deep understanding of how consumer behaviors are changing. Today's consumers are increasingly driven by values like sustainability and ethical sourcing. The once-small market for organic products has exploded into a multi-billion-dollar industry, with shoppers willing to spend more on products that reflect their beliefs. Businesses that meet this demand, whether by ethically sourcing materials or adopting eco-friendly production methods, aren't just surviving; they're thriving.

A great example of this shift can be seen in the fashion industry, where "slow fashion" is challenging the fast fashion model that has dominated for years. As consumers pay more attention to the environmental impact of their purchases, brands that focus on sustainable materials and fair labor practices are gaining popularity. Companies like Patagonia and Allbirds have successfully carved out their places by promoting transparency and sustainability, turning consumer values into profitable business models. Spotting these shifts can lead to fantastic opportunities for those who are aware.

As we move from spotting emerging markets to the technological breakthroughs that drive these changes, it's crucial to recognize the immense impact technology has on market dynamics. The digital revolution has opened up a world of possibilities, transforming industries in ways we couldn't have imagined just a decade ago.

Artificial intelligence (AI) is a prime example of this. It's not just a trendy term; it's a game-changer that's reshaping how we interact with technology and with each other. From improving customer service with chatbots to optimizing supply chains through predictive analytics, AI is creating new markets and opportunities across various sectors. Businesses that use AI to streamline operations or enhance customer experiences can gain a significant advantage.

Blockchain technology is another innovation that is changing the economic landscape. While it started with cryptocurrencies, its uses have expanded dramatically. Industries like finance, healthcare, and logistics are now exploring how blockchain can improve transparency, security, and efficiency. For example, in supply chain management, blockchain can provide a secure record of transactions, ensuring authenticity and cutting down on fraud. Companies that embrace these technologies early can position themselves as leaders in their fields, paving the way for future growth and success.

E-commerce has also become a massive force, changing how we do business. The pandemic sped up a trend that was already happening, as more consumers turned to online shopping out of necessity. Businesses that adapted quickly, whether by enhancing their digital platforms or embracing direct-to-consumer sales, reaped the rewards. In this fast-moving market, the ability to recognize and respond to technological changes is crucial for those looking to seize opportunities and remain competitive.

However, while technological advancements create many opportunities, they can also lead to disruptions. Industries that resist new technologies risk falling behind, as seen with traditional retail struggling against e-commerce. The key is not only recognizing emerging technologies but also figuring out how to use them to create value.

Global events can also greatly influence market dynamics, often presenting unexpected opportunities for those who stay alert and ready to adapt. The COVID-19 pandemic is a perfect example of how rapidly markets can transform. While the pandemic initially hit many sectors hard, it also created a chance for others to flourish. Companies that offered remote work solutions, telehealth services, or e-learning platforms found themselves in high demand, showing how adaptability during a crisis can lead to surprising growth.

Geopolitical changes add another layer of complexity, affecting supply chains and consumer behavior. Ongoing trade tensions between countries can disrupt established markets, but they can also open doors for new players. For instance, as countries look to lessen their dependency on foreign goods, local manufacturers may find opportunities to step in and fill those gaps. Spotting these shifts enables savvy investors to adjust their portfolios or businesses to capture emerging opportunities.

Think about how smart investors and business owners can use these insights. A business owner noticing the rise of remote work might pivot their offerings to cater to this new reality. Whether that means developing software to improve collaboration or creating ergonomic home office furniture, adapting to the changing needs of consumers is essential.

Financial markets also reward those who can anticipate changes. Investors who keep a close eye on global events and technological advancements can position themselves to benefit from emerging trends.

For example, the stock prices of travel companies plummeted when the pandemic hit, but those who saw the potential for recovery when vaccinations became available might have jumped at the chance to invest during a low point.

The key takeaway here is that spotting opportunities requires a mix of awareness, foresight, and flexibility. It's about not just understanding where the market is headed but also being open to change and ready to pivot when necessary. By using insights gained from identifying emerging markets, analyzing tech innovations, and tracking global trends, individuals and businesses can set themselves up for success, even in uncertain times.

Ultimately, the economics world is like a constantly changing puzzle. It consists of pieces that can fit together in surprising ways, revealing glimpses of the future if we're willing to pay attention. By learning to spot these opportunities early, we not only set ourselves up for success but also contribute to a more innovative and resilient economy. The future is filled with potential, and for those who are on the lookout, it's also a chance to make their mark.

Personal Finance: Using Supply and Demand Insights in Daily Life

Life is all about choices, and each choice comes with its own consequences—

especially when it involves managing our money. Every day, we face decisions that can either help us reach our financial goals or lead us into unnecessary struggles. While the ideas of supply and demand might sound like something only found in economics classes or stock market discussions, they are actually quite relevant to our everyday lives. Knowing how supply and demand work can be a valuable skill, helping us make smarter choices about our finances, whether we're grocery shopping, negotiating our salaries, or planning for retirement.

Let's picture a stroll through a typical grocery store. As you wander through the produce section, you might notice that strawberries are much pricier in January than they are in June. Ever wonder why? The answer is rooted in the basics of supply and demand. In winter, strawberries aren't in season in many places, which means there aren't many available. As a result, prices go up because people still crave those delicious berries, even if it means spending more. On the other hand, when summer comes and local farms are overflowing with strawberries, the supply increases, and prices drop. This simple pattern of changing prices based on how much is available is a great example of supply and demand in action, and we can use this knowledge to our advantage in various ways.

Now, think about how this understanding can help with your grocery budget. If you know that certain foods are cheaper at specific times of the year, you can plan your meals around that. Buying in-season fruits and vegetables not only saves you money but also gives you the freshest and tastiest options. The same idea applies to many other products. For example, holiday decorations often go on sale right after the holidays. Knowing the best time to buy can lead to big savings.

There are many ways supply and demand shapes our everyday shopping habits, but it doesn't stop there. Whether you're discussing salary negotiations, bargaining for a car, or figuring out when to buy a big-ticket item like a new TV, having a grasp of these economic concepts can boost your confidence and help you land a better deal. Let's break down these scenarios a bit further.

Take salary negotiations, for example. If you understand the job market, you can make a stronger case for what you deserve. If you're in a field where skilled workers are in high demand but there aren't many qualified candidates, you can confidently request a higher salary. On the flip side, if you're applying for a job in a crowded field where lots of candidates are competing, you might need to adjust your expectations. Knowing the market conditions helps you tailor your requests and approach, so you're not just throwing out random numbers but making informed decisions.

Auto dealerships present another clear example of the impact of supply and demand on financial choices. Imagine you're looking for a new car. If you step into a dealership in January when new models are hitting the market, you might find that last year's cars are heavily discounted. This is a perfect time to snag a great deal. Understanding when supplies change can help you negotiate better prices and decide whether it's smart to buy now or wait for future sales.

Being aware of the cycles of supply and demand also helps when it comes to making major purchases. Whether it's appliances, technology, or even real estate, the timing of your purchase can make a big difference in cost. Seasonal trends often lead to lower prices at certain times of the year. For instance, many stores offer big discounts on home appliances during holiday sales like Labor Day or Black Friday. If you can plan ahead and buy during these times, you could save a lot of money, all thanks to supply and demand dynamics.

Looking beyond immediate purchases, understanding supply and demand is also vital for long-term financial planning. This insight doesn't just apply to daily transactions; it can shape your investment strategies and savings decisions too. Let's talk about how this knowledge can influence your financial future.

When investing, the balance of supply and demand can greatly affect different markets. The real estate market, for example, is known for its ups and downs. Areas where demand exceeds supply often see rapid increases in property values. If you're thinking about investing in real estate, knowing your local market and recognizing when demand is high can lead to smart choices. Buying property in a sought-after neighborhood while prices are still reasonable can be a strategic move that pays off in the long run.

Similarly, the stock market follows the same supply and demand principles. Companies that show strong potential for growth tend to have high demand for their shares, pushing prices up. Smart investors pay attention to market trends to figure out when demand might rise. For example, if a tech company is set to launch an exciting new product, it could be a great time to buy shares before demand—and the stock price—climb. On the other hand, knowing when a market is saturated can help you sidestep trouble—like selling shares before a downturn hits.

This kind of strategic thinking also extends to planning for retirement. People who understand supply and demand can make better choices about where to put their savings. For instance, if everyone is jumping on a popular investment like cryptocurrency or specific stocks, it's wise to dig deeper into why that's happening. Is the demand based on solid fundamentals, or is it just a passing trend? Balancing these insights with a diverse portfolio can help reduce risks and prepare you for whatever the market throws your way.

A key part of long-term financial planning is also recognizing shifts in consumer behavior. There's been a growing demand for sustainable investments, as more people seek ethical options when spending their money. This trend has led to more companies that align with these values, making them attractive to investors. If you notice this trend in sustainability, it could be smart to invest in companies that prioritize environmental and social responsibility. Understanding supply and demand can guide you toward investments that not only match your values but might also lead to good returns.

In the end, the lessons learned from supply and demand go beyond theory. By applying these concepts to your everyday financial choices, you can develop a mindset focused on strategic thinking and informed decisions. This proactive approach helps you navigate the often complicated world of personal finance, so you're ready for both opportunities and challenges that come your way.

As we think about the importance of supply and demand in our lives, remember that knowledge is power. The more we understand the economic factors involved, the better we can make choices that lead to financial stability and growth. Whether it's planning your next grocery trip or laying the groundwork for a secure retirement, using insights from supply and demand can light the way forward.

The connection between economics and personal finance is packed with possibilities for those willing to explore it. By gaining a solid understanding of how supply and demand shape our financial landscape, we not only enhance our decision-making skills but also take control of our financial futures. Being informed means being empowered, and grasping these principles can help us make choices that positively impact our lives. So, the next time you face a financial decision, keep in mind that a little knowledge can go a long way in shaping your economic journey. Make your choices with confidence, equipped with the insights from these timeless principles of supply and demand.

Conclusion

As we conclude our exploration of supply and demand, it's clear that these fundamental principles are the invisible hand guiding our economic world. From the fluctuating prices of everyday goods to the complex dynamics of global markets, the concepts we've discussed are at work all around us.

Armed with this knowledge, you're now better equipped to make informed decisions in your daily life. Whether you're budgeting for groceries, investing in stocks, or simply trying to understand why certain products are priced the way they are, you have the tools to interpret the economic signals that surround you.

Remember, economics isn't just about numbers and graphs – it's about human behavior, choices, and the constant interplay between what we want and what's available. By understanding these principles, you're not just a passive observer of the economy, but an active participant with the power to influence markets through your decisions.

As you move forward, keep your eyes open to the economic forces at play in your world. Challenge yourself to apply what you've learned, and don't be afraid to dig deeper into the fascinating realm of economics. The more you understand, the better prepared you'll be to navigate the ever-changing landscape of our global marketplace.

So, the next time you see a price tag, remember – there's a story behind it, and now you have the key to unlock its secrets. Welcome to your new, economically savvy life!

Alfred Greene

www.ingramcontent.com/pod-product-compliance
Lightning Source LLC
Chambersburg PA
CBHW061342250726

48657CB00004B/1284